THE TRAILMAN'S HANDBOOK

For Navigators and Adventurers

PREMIER EDITION

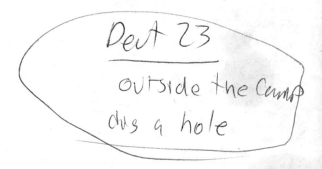

TRAIL LIFE USA®

Belton, South Carolina

THE TRAILMAN'S HANDBOOK by John Burkitt, Editor in Chief
Published by Youth Adventure Program, Incorporated, dba Worthy Trailman Press
10612 Augusta Rd
Belton, SC 29627
www.TrailLifeUSA.com

Unless otherwise noted, all Scripture quotations are from King James Version.

Interior design: Anna Jelstrom
Cover design and illustration: Ken Raney

International Standard Book Number: ISBN# 978-0-9912316-1-4

Premier edition, second printing.

17 — 9876543

Printed in the United States of America.

Dedicated to the Adventure
of Growing in the Image of God
in God's Great Outdoors

ACKNOWLEDGMENTS

This work is the result of centuries of man hours spent in the outdoors where Nature herself is the harshest editor. The following individuals have contributed substantially to the book you see before you: Dr. John Burkitt, John Slagboom, Dr. Kip Haggerty, Laura Burton, Stewart W. Nolan, Jr. (representing the Catholic Committee), David Servin, and Mark Hancock. Also providing editing were Richard Mathews and John Stemberger. Assistance with Cooking was provided by Brian Boone and Claude Freaner. We also recognize Patti Garibay and the American Heritage Girls for their support and contribution of the program concepts of their organization.

The seminal work of many leaders living and dead in the Boy Scouts of America is gratefully acknowledged, especially that of William "Green Bar Bill" Hillcourt whose warm, conversational prose captured the beauty of growing up so eloquently.

SENIOR EDITORIAL STAFF
Project director: David Servin
Editor in Chief: John Burkitt
Project coordination: Mark Hancock
Design and layout: John Burkitt, Anna Jelstrom
Proofreaders: Lynne Riday, Amy Davis

FROM THE EDITOR

When you start a good fire, you don't hold your match under the biggest log. You start with the smallest tinder. Bit by bit the leaves catch the twigs on fire and the twigs ignite the branches. Before long even the largest logs are burning brightly.

It's like that with most things in life. Your basic outdoor skills may not come easily at first. That's alright ... really. What you see in this Handbook is designed to challenge you, for any skill that is not challenging is not worth having. The simple skills will help you tackle progressively harder tasks and before long you'll be confident in the great outdoors. This will happen sooner than you think.

From there you will continue to grow in wisdom and character through the awards of Trail Life USA. Then it's on to other challenges, other opportunities for development that will keep you growing throughout your whole earthly life. Growth is all about leaving behind "child-ISH" while remaining "child-LIKE," a point Jesus made when He spoke of entering the Kingdom of Heaven as a child.

The editorial staff has shared in this Handbook what worked for us on our journey. Yet you are also on a very personal adventure and as you head into the unknown, never be afraid to try new things. The trick to being successful is to measure those new ideas against the yardstick of the traditional values that have helped generations face new challenges and find new horizons with courage, compassion and grace. As you journey forth, may God give you vision and the courage to use it.

Dr. John H. Burkitt

WALK WORTHY!

CONTENTS

INTRODUCTION

JOIN THE ADVENTURE!

Life is an adventure! With a can-do attitude and the skills to keep you safe and comfortable, you'll make the most of it, taking on new challenges and claiming new rewards around each hill, across each valley, and around each bend in the river.

The American adventure was started by explorers. It was carried on by settlers. It was defended by soldiers and tilled by farmers. It was taken from an idea to a real and wonderful place stretching from the Atlantic to the Pacific, from Canada to Mexico. Now it is yours, and you should carry on the adventure with an enthusiasm worthy of our great nation.

The outdoor adventure will teach you important things about life and living it. Nothing beats waking up in a tent you pitched yourself, then sitting down to a breakfast cooked on an open fire in God's great outdoors. The wilderness will challenge you, and sometimes it will throw you a curve, but it will also be your home. When you learn how to live in it, good times lay ahead that you will never forget. Whether you walk the misty pines of Maine, cross the open prairies of Kansas, wade the wild surf of Florida, or admire the blue sky of Montana, it will be your heritage to enjoy and protect.

The spiritual adventure is the greatest one, and it's the one that never ends. As a baby, you were the center of your own small universe. Then one day you realized that the faces over you were other people with thoughts and feelings just like yours. No longer were you alone! The greatest discovery of all is to realize that you are never truly alone. As night falls in your camp and you see the vast starry sky above you, take a moment to consider that the wise and loving God Who made it also wants to live in your heart. The Lord gave you a lifetime in this world of beauty and wonder. Make every day worthwhile, using your opportunities well and seeking to know and do His will.

What can be better than sharing the adventure with other like-minded boys who will help you each step of the way? In your Troop, you'll find great friends who appreciate the blessings of God, the greatness of America, the boy you are today, and the man you will be tomorrow. Some of these boys will be friends for life, but all of them will live on in the happy memories you make.

Well, what are you waiting for?

Programs of Trail Life USA

The Woodlands Trail, with a focus on gaining *knowledge*, is a family program for boys: Kindergarten and First Grade (Foxes), Second and Third Grade (Hawks), and Fourth and Fifth Grade (Mountain Lions) that involves the family in fun and inspiring activities.

WOODLANDS TRAIL

The Navigators Program, with an emphasis on *understanding*, is an inspirational and richly rewarding program for Sixth to Eighth Grade boys who seek to achieve mental, moral, emotional, and physical fitness through adventures in God's great outdoors with the guidance of Trailman ideals.

NAVIGATORS PROGRAM

The Adventurers Program, designed to foster *wisdom*, is a high adventure, high energy program for Ninth to Twelfth Grade boys who want to take ownership of activities, being intimately involved with every aspect of planning and implementing them in a democratic environment.

ADVENTURERS PROGRAM

Delta Life is an optional program concentrating on outreach for Sixth to Twelfth Grade boys seeking to get the most out of their time in the Navigators and Adventurers Program years.

The Guidon Program, with a focus on *life*, is an outdoor adventure program for 18-25 year old Christian young men and women. Under church mentors, young adults hold each other to a "higher" Christian standard and purity in a world where those virtues are not that common.

WHERE TO START

- If you're a boy who is at least 11 years old and not yet 18, great! Go to a Troop in your area and introduce yourself to Trail Life USA leaders and boys. The Trailmen help you find your way, including sending you to the website where you can learn more and register.
- You will be asked to show the *Trailman sign*, give the *Trailman handshake*, and to say the Pledge of Allegiance while giving the *Trailman salute*. All those things are taught in this Handbook. Your new Trailmen friends will help you, too.
- Being a Trailman is a privilege, not a right. Show the Trailmaster that you understand and accept the *Trailman Oath* and the *Outdoor Pledge*.
- After you have done these things and turned in your paperwork, you will have a Leader Conference designed to help you get the most out of the program.
- Welcome aboard! As a new Trailman, you can experience life to the fullest with your new friends and proudly wear the uniform.

THE PLEDGE OF ALLEGIANCE

The flag of the United States is a symbol of the freedom and justice we enjoy. In 1892, Francis Bellamy wrote the Pledge of Allegiance to help citizens show respect to the flag. In 1954 the words "under God" were added to the Pledge to thank God for the blessings we have as Americans.

I pledge allegiance to the Flag
of the United States of America,
and to the Republic for which it stands,
one Nation under God, indivisible,
with liberty and justice for all.

THE TRAILMAN SIGN, SALUTE AND HANDSHAKE

Wolves howl to recognize their own. Foxes recognize familiar smells. Bears look for marks on trees, and whales have distinctive songs. If you're a Trailman, you'll find it easier to identify yourself to others using the Trailman sign, salute, and handshake. Along with your uniform, these actions identify you as a member of a great brotherhood.

The Trailman sign is made with the right hand held open, palm forward, raising your right arm with your elbow at a right angle.

Trailman sign

Bring the right hand up, palm down, until your forefinger touches the brim of your hat or the tip of your right eyebrow for the Trailman salute.

Trailman salute

The Trailman handshake is like a regular right-handed handshake, except that you reach further forward and grasp the other's wrist.

Trailman handshake

THE TRAILMAN OATH

On my honor I will do my best
to serve God and my country;
to respect authority;
to be a good steward of creation;
and to treat others as I want to be treated.

Your honor is something like the wind. You can't see the wind, but you can see when the trees move and the clouds go by. You can't see honor, but you can spot it quickly by watching the things it does. Honor is that quality that makes you keep promises and do the right thing whether or not someone else is watching you.

Doing your best does not end at the edge of your comfort zone. Most people never discover their best because they become rather pleased with themselves at good or better. You discover your best by continuing to push yourself with new challenges. You will find that your best gets even better with study and practice.

Serving God and your country is not just a duty, it's a privilege. Understanding that God and America need your unique talents and dedication gives you a wonderful feeling of belonging.

Respecting authority is both a responsibility and a skill. You have a responsibility to obey just orders, and you should use discernment to act within the framework of your Christian faith.

A good steward of Creation does not wantonly destroy or waste the blessings God gives. That includes everything from taking care of your own health and upkeep of your house and yard to preventing forest fires and keeping the air and water pure. A steward is one that takes care of things for their rightful owner, and that owner is God.

Treating other people as you want to be treated is also called the Golden Rule. It was taught by Jesus Christ, who advised us to do unto others as we would have them do unto us.

THE TRAILMAN MOTTO

Walk Worthy!

Anything worth doing has certain standards you should strive to meet. A story needs a plot, a car needs a motor, and a life well-led needs certain qualities of decency, accomplishment, and service to others. As you walk the trail, seek to uphold high standards.

> *"... that you may walk worthy of the Lord, fully pleasing Him, being fruitful in every good work and increasing in the knowledge of God..."*
> Colossians 1:10 (NKJV)

THE TRAILMAN STANDARD

The Trailman's Standard is a staff used by a Trailman. Like you, the wood of the staff started out small and helpless, a seedling. Like you, it grew tall and sturdy, capable of supporting itself and others. The Trailman Standard is your partner, and it comes to you unadorned, awaiting the achievements you will fasten to it the same way experiences and achievements become a part of you. Like Trailmen themselves, the Standards have much in common while also possessing a distinct character that becomes more unique with the passage of time and miles.

THE OUTDOORS

God made the world and said that it was good. It is up to you to keep it that way. Use low-impact hiking and camping techniques. While you are showing respect for nature, be sure you also show respect for private property and the rights of other people who are out enjoying nature. Always leave a campsite as good—or better—than you found it.

YOUR UNIFORM

The Trailman uniform is designed for real boys who have real adventures. It is durable and attractive by design, but it will last longer and look better if you take proper care of it. Trailmen wear their Trail shirt, Travel/Meeting shirt, or Troop/Ceremony shirt proudly. Your Leaders will instruct you on which shirt to wear when.

The uniform shows others that you care about God, America, and adventurous living. As a symbol of the good will and ideals of Trail Life USA, it should be worn at Troop events, but it should not be worn at political events, non-troop fund-raisers, or any place or activity that does not reflect well on the organization or its non-political nature. This uniform should not be worn by anyone who is not a member in good standing or otherwise put on display in a disrespectful manner.

All Trailman ranks, awards, and achievement badges are earned honors; and badges of office are elected honors. Your uniform should display all honors to which you are currently entitled, and they should be neatly and correctly worn. Badges of office should be removed once your term expires. If you want to wear more badges for earned honors, go out and earn them honestly so you can wear them proudly.

> The uniform shows others that you care about God, America, and adventurous living.

There are times when it's OK to wear a Troop or camp T-shirt with the uniform pants or shorts. For certain activities where you're sure to get muddy or wrinkled, you might want to try on jeans and pass the uniform altogether. Your Leaders will advise you when activities call for more casual dress.

LEADER CONFERENCE

After you have completed the joining requirements, you will have a talk with your Leader about Troop safety and what lies ahead on the advancement trail. It helps you to understand where you are and where you are going. It also gives the Leader some idea of how well boys are enjoying the program and what can be done to improve it for everyone.

For each new rank or award you complete, you'll have an Advancement Conference. That's because you are not just growing on the outside, you're also growing on the inside in your heart and mind. Your Leader watches your progress and listens to your opinions to make sure you are getting the most out of the program.

Navigators Program

6th –8th grade

NAVIGATOR RANKS

Recruit Trailman - The Recruit has taken his first big step as a Trailman.

Able Trailman - The Able Trailman is truly an able man. He knows how to hike safely and comfortably and handle a lot of situations that might come up. These skills are the foundation for the next ranks.

Ready Trailman - The Ready Trailman is ready for whatever happens. He has a full set of camping skills and does his fair share of the work as well as the fun. After you have earned the highest rank in Navigators you have the confidence and experience to teach skills to newer members and give back to the Troop some of the help that you got when you were starting out. As the Bible teaches, those who would be great must be servants of others.

ADVENTURER AWARDS

Journey – A Journey Trailman is at the head of a higher Adventurer Trail, one of leadership. As you take this trail, Christ should be your guide. He is the way, the truth, and the life. The Bible tells us He is a lamp unto your feet and a light unto your path.

Horizon – A Horizon Trailman still looks back to the younger boys and helps them with their skills, but he also looks ahead to the Freedom Award and seeks to help the Troop succeed and to help Freedom candidates with their Freedom projects. You'll not only be useful to the Troop, you'll be learning valuable lessons about life that will pay off time and again when you are a man.

You will come across many new ideas and opportunities on your way to manhood. Some of them lead to great things, others to disaster. You will show your wisdom as you avoid the pitfalls and keep your heart and mind headed upward, developing the image of God in you, and becoming the man you were born to be.

Freedom – A Freedom Rangeman understands and appreciates his freedom as a gift given all mankind by God. He also understands that the chance to enjoy that freedom was bought by the hard work, courage, and sacrifices of men just like himself.

Attaining the highest award in Trail Life USA requires a special service project that demonstrates the skills and ideals you learned in your Troop. It will be challenging, but you can rise to that challenge and help freedom ring in your town, your country, and your world.

YOUR PATROL

A patrol is a group of six to eight boys that are like a small family inside the big family of your Troop. You have an elected patrol leader and junior patrol leader to keep things moving, and you can have fun in friendly competition with other patrols in your Troop.

Patrol members camp together, play together, and learn together. And if you have a mind to, you can work to be the best patrol in your Troop.

A certain part of each Troop meeting may be set aside for patrols to meet separately. At times like this you can work on patrol flags, plan menus, and even make plans for patrol outings.

One patrol in your Troop may be set aside for new boys and assigned an older boy as a Patrol Leader or a Trail Guide to help teach the important first skills leading to the Ready Trailman rank.

If you just joined as a Navigator, you will have a lot of fun in your first days as a Trailman, but you will also want to reach Ready Trailman soon.

> A patrol is a group of six to eight boys inside your Troop.

YOUR TROOP

The Troop is made up of all the patrols, boys holding the elected offices of First Officer, Second Officer, and Quartermaster, and your adult leaders, headed up by the Trailmaster and Advisor.

The Troop is your extended family, and it meets once a week and usually has an outdoor activity once a month. It is large enough to tackle big tasks and plan exciting outings. These may be people that you already know from church or school, or they might be totally new to you. You'll find that they share a love of adventure with you, and that's a great thing to have in common.

While the Trailmaster signs paperwork, provides leadership and guidance, runs the Navigators meetings, and steps in from time to time, it is the First Officer who runs Adventurers meetings and, together with his Second Officer, Patrol Leaders, and Junior Patrol Leaders, conducts a patrol leaders council to plan outings and see what went right—and wrong—with activities. These youth leaders are elected. You will always get to vote, and it makes sense that if you want to hold office, you should be the sort of boy you would vote for yourself!

The Troop is made up of all the patrols.

GO FOR IT!

The Adventuring trail to the Freedom Award looks very long after you've only taken a few first steps. Yet, almost before you know it, your uniform shirt will tell an exciting story of progress and experience. Fix your sights on the Freedom Award today!

August is laughing across the sky,

Laughing while paddle, canoe and I,

Drift, drift, where the hills uplift

On either side of the current swift.

— Kirk Wipper

TRAIL LIFE USA™

JOINING REQUIREMENTS

Traditions:
- Memorize and agree to live by the Trailman Oath.
- Memorize the Trailman Motto.
- Demonstrate the Trailman sign and describe when to use it.
- Demonstrate the Trailman salute and describe when to use it.
- Demonstrate the Trailman handshake.
- Give your Patrol Leader's name, patrol name, and patrol yell.

Citizenship:
- Memorize the Pledge of Allegiance.
- Demonstrate properly folding the American flag.

Leader Conference:
- Discuss Troop safety.
- Discuss advancement program.

WELCOME ABOARD!

RESPONSIBILITIES

LEADERSHIP

Leadership skills are important for everyone because we are *all* leaders. Always you are leading yourself, and you also lead others by example. Sometimes, you will be placed in a formal position of leadership, and if you are wise, you won't wait till the last minute to prepare yourself for success. Start now by working on the **four selves: self-respect, self-control, self-reliance**, and **self-worth**. Think of these as the poles that hold up the tent of your character. Take away one, and the tent sags. Take away two, and the tent collapses.

Self-Respect

Self-respect does not mean being stuck up or conceited. It's a sort of contentment you get when your conscience is not bothering you and it has no real reason to try.

If you don't know what that feels like, or it's been a long time since you felt that way, pray about it and look at ways you can make up for the shortcomings of the past and be a better man in the future. Once you've experienced that freedom, you'll go to great lengths to hold on to it.

You gain self-respect when you do what you know is right rather than always doing what pleases you or makes you more popular.

Self-Control

Self-control is not necessarily the same thing as self-denial. It's more like a truce you call when your long-term needs and short-term wants are at war. Needs and wants are both important, but they have to work together to achieve great things. Self-control helps you balance these.

Try a little experiment. Take an empty can and fill it to the rim with large rocks. When you think it's completely full and nothing else will go in, get some small gravel and see how much can go into the spaces between the large rocks. Impressive,

> Needs and wants are both important, but they have to work together to achieve great things. Self-control helps you balance these.

huh? But you're not through yet.

You can take a whole handful of sand and put it into the spaces between the rocks and gravel. And just when you think it's over, try pouring a glass of water in and see if the whole thing won't fit!

Large rocks, gravel, sand, and water are all important, but if you don't put the large rocks in first, you won't have room for them later.

Those large rocks are what are truly important in life—God, family, friends, and your country. The small pebbles are your minor goals. The sand is your hobbies and interests. The water is when you just want to do something for fun or hang out with your friends.

That's why self-control does not necessarily mean self-denial. Quite often the fellow with more self-control has more good things to enjoy than the one who lacks discipline and restraint!

Self-control means you do what you *should* do so you can do what you want to do.

Self-Reliance

Do you like reading stories about people with super powers? Perhaps you have given some thought to what abilities you would like to wield against the forces of evil.

You might as well forget having super powers. Those make for good reading, but they are hardly practical. On the other hand, there are a lot of ordinary powers which would do the world—and you—a lot more good a lot more often. Whether it is cooking your own meal over a campfire or having a real command of first aid, it's a great feeling to have

new things, do your best, and give everything you do your best shot.

Self-Worth

Self-worth sounds a lot like self-esteem, but they are not exactly the same. Imagine taking an item you want to sell to an appraiser. The appraiser will give you some idea of the item's value. You have worth as well, and self-worth is something you develop from knowing that God put you in this world for a reason and that he will equip you to carry out that role and find your purpose. As a young man made in the image of God, you are important—so important that Christ died on the cross for you. You should acknowledge that importance by living a healthful and moral life, taking care of the blessings God gave you, and wisely pursuing the opportunities he sends you. You should acknowledge your importance to the people who love and depend upon you by being the best you can be. You should acknowledge the God who made you by seeking to please him and doing his will. Being loved, needed, and counted upon feels great, but it is also a responsibility. The only question should be if it's worth the price. Most assuredly it is!

skills and not to have to constantly rely on other people to help you.

That's not to say that every person should try to learn every skill that might be useful someday. God gave everyone different talents, and there are some things you'll learn to do better than most of your friends. Other things that seem to come naturally to most people may be a challenge for you. That's all right, really. Together as a troop, and later as an employee or family man, you'll combine your unique talents with the talents of others and make the world a better place for doing so. The important question to ask yourself is, "What is my potential and how can I reach it?" The only way to answer that question is to try

THE PROPER ATTITUDE

When you realize that a leader is giving you the gift of guidance, you will not resent being a follower. In turn, as you lead others, you will not be arrogant or prideful, but will feel the joy of giving guidance to others. They will naturally accept that kind of leadership in the spirit in which it is given.

People tend to follow leaders they like and admire. If you want people to like and admire you, you should be the sort of person who can like and admire himself. If you cannot command self-respect, you won't command respect in others.

You gain self-respect from doing what you know is right rather than always doing what pleases you, or doing something just because it is the popular thing to do!

Remember that there are no unimportant jobs. Whether you are leading a group of backpackers through the wilderness or teaching a new boy to tie a bowline, do it as well as you can.

Think of leadership as a wind-up clock: There are lots of gears and levers inside, and some of them look more important than others. But when any one of them is removed the clock stops running. If you would repair a clock, treat all of its moving parts with the same care. Do the same thing with the people that count on you.

ROLE MODELS

A role model is someone whom people look up to and aspire to imitate. If you want to be a great explorer like Admiral Byrd or a great artist like Renoir, those people are your role models. We also look up to people we think do ordinary things in great ways.

Ideally, everyone should have good role models and try to be a good role model to others. This is all too often not the case. If we let desire for popularity, wealth, or power take a more important role in our lives than honesty, kindness, or wisdom, it is easy to make bad choices of role models for ourselves and to be a bad role model for others.

In Adventuring there are many things you can say to your fellow troop and patrol members, but actions really do speak louder than words. Leadership by example is the gold standard—you should settle for nothing less.

PERSEVERANCE

Perseverance is just a fancy way of saying, "Never give up!" It's a very important skill of leadership because your enthusiasm for a long project will change daily, like the weather. The people who reach the finish line are the ones that keep on going when they start to feel tired and discouraged. Remember, almost any project you begin will start with a burst of enthusiasm and a can-do attitude. Your ability to get through the boring or discouraging parts will depend on how determined you are to see it through. Determined people—the people who persevere—will see it through.

ADVANCE PREPARATION

You expect the success of your campout to depend on having the right equipment. Your success as a leader also depends on having the right equipment and making advance preparation. Matching the right person to the right job is essential for good morale and mission success. Either find someone with the necessary skills, or train someone until they can handle the responsibility with grace and good humor.

While you are about this, be sure to train yourself. Keep track of what worked and what went wrong. Keep an eye on successful leaders and use your powers of observation to spot what makes them successful. Don't just imitate successful people; adopt their talents as your own and make them uniquely yours. Before long, other people in your troop may be watching YOU.

> The best way to discover your real potential is to keep challenging yourself. Aim each time you do something to do it a bit better than you did it the last time.

SETTING GOALS

Setting a lofty goal may make you feel like a hero or a saint. Yet if you don't want to set yourself up for failure, know what is within your grasp and then set your mind and heart to get it. The best way to discover your real potential is to keep challenging yourself. Aim each time you do something to do it a bit better than you did it the last time. Your best work is nothing to be ashamed of, even if it is not as good as someone else's. He may do something better than you can, but chances are there's something you can do better than he can. That's what makes you a person—a unique combination of strengths and weaknesses.

Self-improvement stands on two legs. First, you should learn to recognize your strengths and work on improving them, looking for useful outlets for your own creativity, determination, and insight. Second, you can also put some effort into minimizing your weaknesses. They may never become your strong point, but you never know that one of them might be a strength that simply needed more attention!

One way to get to know yourself better is to try new things on campouts. Don't let the fear of being embarrassed hold you back.

Remember that the only stupid questions are the ones you refuse to ask! Becoming the best you can be is a wonderful feeling, and achieving your goals gives you a great sense of accomplishment.

Have a way to measure success

in leadership—define it in things you can see or touch. If you want to "improve" a trail system, success may mean a smooth course free of obstacles and covered with an inch of pine mulch. You cannot measure the word "success" or even "improve," but you can certainly measure pine mulch! Once you are underway, keep an eye on your progress toward your goal.

Halfway through the time you have allotted to achieve your goal, you should stop and ask yourself if you are halfway through with the job. If not, you'll have time to retool your efforts and pick up the pace.

Being able to measure success in this way will help you later on in life. Taking a project from an idea to a series of steps is an important business skill.

LEADERSHIP IN THE TROOP

Troop elections are a great way to get experience with leadership, both by holding an office yourself and by voting for other people. After a "popularity contest" or two, you'll realize that the boy with the best sense of humor or the best free throw does not necessarily make the best leader.

There are three things you look for. First, you want a person who is **willing** to do the job. Without the right attitude, a person is worthless as a leader. Second, you want someone who is **able** to do the job. To a degree your Trailmaster or Advisor will handle this for you by drawing up a list of eligible boys. Third, you want someone who is **ready** to

STYLES OF LEADERSHIP

You can try to be **popular** by letting your patrol members vote on everything. Doing what everyone else wants is a sure way to become popular—until you run into trouble. You can try to be **masterful** by choosing what seems right to you and barking out orders (good luck with that!). The best leaders are **unifying**, harnessing the experience and enthusiasm of the team while giving it clarity and direction. Remember, leadership is a service to others.

work. Having constant schedule conflicts does not make someone a bad person, but it does render that person an ineffective leader.

It goes without saying—but let's say it: A boy starts his leadership position with less experience and ends it with more. Be patient with newly elected officers; when it is your turn, they may well return the favor. Youth leaders are a work in progress, and your decision to be a better leader will serve you for the rest of your life.

Patrol Leader

This is not the highest ranking job in the troop but it gets most of the work done. Patrol Leaders are Adventurer Program youths who keep things moving and guide and lead the other patrol members to make sure duty rosters get carried out. If one Trailman in the patrol is overwhelmed with too much to do and another is standing around with his hands in his pockets, his Patrol Leader knows what to do!

Patrol Leaders are also patrol members and they do their share of the work. After all, being a contributing patrol member is part of leadership, by showing leadership through example. A Patrol Leader who is the king of

his castle and orders his peasants about will be in for some unpleasant surprises when work does not get done and no one wants to make him First Officer come election time. A good Patrol Leader understands that "we" do things together to make Adventuring happen. There is no "I" or "U" in Patrol Leader.

Patrol Leaders are members of the Patrol Leaders Council and keep the patrol members' wants in mind as outings and changes in procedure are planned.

Junior Patrol Leader

This is a great starting job for troop leadership. Junior Patrol Leaders

are Navigator Program youths who set a good example to follow and give advice when Navigators meet separately from the whole troop. He is also a member of the Patrol Leaders Council.

First Officer

This is a highly visible job as it is the highest ranking office in your troop. The First Officer runs troop meetings under the watchful eye of the Advisor and, during joint events with Navigators, the Trailmaster. He also chairs the Patrol Leaders Council. Being elected First Officer is the highest vote of confidence you can receive from your fellow Trailmen.

Because the First Officer sets the tone for troop meetings and Patrol Leaders Council meetings, it is important to know how to have a little fun but keep things moving. With the whole troop as your "captive audience," there is a tendency to feel like this is your moment in the spotlight. However, it is the troop that should be in the spotlight. You are not simply there as yourself, you are also the voice of the troop, and the way you behave gives the troop dignity and professionalism.

As First Officer, you are the "point man" for concerns of the other boys in your troop. If there is a problem you can't fix, you take it to the Advisor yourself. If it's a matter that requires the use of authority, the Advisor will back up your decisions unless they are downright unreasonable. You are, after all, the highest ranking Trailman. You will also support the decisions of the patrol leaders under you if you think they are fair and reasonable.

Second Officer

This is a great place to serve your troop, gain valuable leadership knowledge and pause and catch your breath on your way up the ladder to First Officer. You not only substitute when the First Officer cannot be there, you also learn from him, attend the Patrol Leaders Council meetings, and help the First Officer supervise the troop on outings and during meetings.

Quartermaster

The Quartermaster keeps charge of troop equipment and food and, while he is in charge of objects rather than people, he is very important to the people who use equipment and troop library resources. In other words, the Quartermaster is important to **everyone**.

YOUR ADULT LEADERS

Adults leaders are not there to be bosses. They counsel youth leadership and provide guidance.

They believe in the boy you are today and the man you will be tomorrow. They accept and appreciate the Lordship of Jesus Christ and help bring out the image of God in you.

Troopmaster

The Troopmaster oversees the operation of the entire unit, from the Woodlands Trail all the way through Adventurers.

Trailmaster

The leading adult in your Navigators troop is a man of good character who is at least 21 years of age, is bound by the Statement of Faith and Values, and agrees to live by the Trailman Oath.

Your Trailmaster will give you trustworthy advice and help you succeed.

Advisor

The Advisor guides the youth leaders in the Adventurers program and ensures health, safety, and other guidelines are being met in all proposed activities. While his

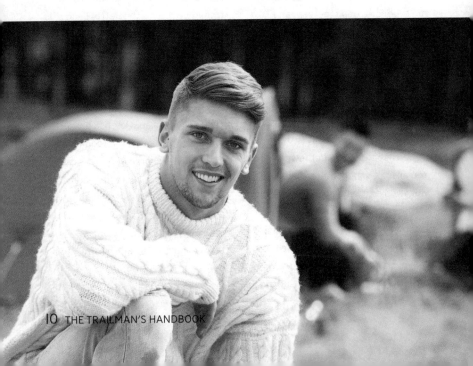

opinion is valued, his main function is to ensure that approved Adventurers activities are carried out safely and effectively.

Trail Guides

These adult leaders are at least 18 years old and have to meet the same requirements as the Trailmaster and Advisor. They are there to help you along the trail.

Trail Guides may have specialized assignments such as working with the new boys, helping with rank advancement, or setting up camp.

Troop Committee

A group of concerned adults who are responsible for the smooth operation of your troop, keeping track of such things as advancement, transportation, finances, and fund-raising.

CEREMONIES

At any given moment what we know and what we feel may be quite different. Ceremonies help our understanding and our emotions come together to highlight important moments along the Adventuring Trail. A well-planned ceremony gives the occasion the dignity and drama it deserves.

Opening Ceremony

A Troop meeting should always include posting the colors with all hands at attention, reciting the Pledge of Allegiance, and giving the Trailman Oath. How precisely this is carried out is left at the discretion of the week's patrol, but it should be approved by the Trailmaster or Advisor.

Closing Ceremony

We recommend that you close the meeting with a benediction. "Benediction" is a fancy word from Latin that means, "speak well" or "good word." You might want to develop a special benediction for your troop."

Presentation of Ranks and Awards

The local unit should use its own creativity in planning the presentation of ranks and awards. One thing that should be avoided is just calling people up to the podium, handing them the emblem, and shaking their hand.

Make sure you properly acknowledge these advancements. To save time, you might want to present to a group, but still recognize the effort involved.

Be more concerned
with your **character**
than your **reputation**,
because your **character**
is what you really are,
while your **reputation**
is merely what others
think you are.

—John Wooden

2 CITIZENSHIP

You belong to several different families. Like your blood relatives, the families of community, nation, and world give you certain rights and expect certain responsibilities in return. The name for these rights and responsibilities is *citizenship.*

PAST, PRESENT, AND FUTURE

As a Trailman, you want to enjoy your rights and uphold your responsibilities like the good young man you are. Doing this means understanding citizenship. It means living in the past, the present, and the future all at once. Yes, your past (heritage) is with you today and helps make you who and what you are. Your present (opportunity) is about making a difference for good using the options and resources you have today. Of course, as you pursue present opportunities, you also look to the future (vision) with your dreams and goals for yourself and the world around you.

GOVERNMENT

When people live together, they must have certain rules to settle disputes and certain people with the authority to enforce those rules fairly on everyone. This process is *government.*

Most every government in the world also has other functions, ranging from health care to public transportation to armed forces. Citizens of those countries have private property that they paid for themselves but they also have public property that was paid for by everyone through taxes. Where governments differ widely today is in how these functions are controlled and how much power the ordinary citizen has over the process.

Once it was fairly common to have kings and emperors rule over people. Their word was the law and there was little—if anything—that the ordinary citizen could do about unpopular laws. Around 2,500 years ago, the ancient Greek city of Athens started a new form of government called democracy that allowed all citizens to vote

The Constitution of the United States is a legal document that gives some direction to the way laws are made and enforced. It provides you certain civil rights that cannot be taken away from you by your neighbors.

on the laws that would govern them. "Democracy" is a Greek word that means "rule by the people." Since Athens was rather small, that was fairly easy to do.

This kind of democracy is impractical in large modern nations. Even with today's Internet and social media, the number and complexity of the issues involved would take too much time for the average citizen to spare. That's why America is a republic, a place where people select lawmakers to do this important work for them.

Unlike the pure democracy of Athens, we Americans have a constitution to prevent the majority of the people from ruling over the minority. The Constitution of the United States is a legal document that gives some direction to the way laws are made and enforced. It provides you certain civil rights that cannot be taken away from you by your neighbors. No one can force you to move out of your neighborhood because they don't like your religion, your opinion, your national origin, or the color of your skin. You have many other rights as well. These rights give society a degree of stability and prevent large groups of people from making life hard for smaller groups.

THE AMERICAN SUCCESS STORY

Imagine how exciting it was to find that the world had twice as many lands, twice as many peoples, and twice the opportunity! It was like getting an extra Earth.

Many people came to the New World excited at the chance to discover worldly riches, and some of them did become very wealthy. However, the settlers that made the greatest difference were looking for freedom, especially the freedom to worship God as they saw fit. Those people found the greatest and longest lasting treasure America had to offer.

In 1776, thirteen colonies owned by Great Britain decided that the government of King George III was not adequately protecting their rights. After much thought and debate, they decided to unite and become an independent nation.

Building that new-found American

freedom to the level we enjoy today and defending it in a series of wars required a lot of courage, sacrifice, and hard work. Not all of the battles were fought with foreigners, and not all were fought on a battlefield; some of the freedoms we take for granted, such as the outlawing of slavery and the rights of women to vote, were fought inside the United States with citizens on both sides of the issue.

It is often said that eternal vigilance is the price of liberty. That simply means that the cost of freedom is not free. Never take our American freedoms for granted.

ISSUES AND ANSWERS

You have a device in your home that will help you see the future—it's called a mirror. When you look into it, you'll see someone who hopefully will learn from the successes and mistakes of the past and set a wise course for the future that you—and those who follow you—must walk. While you are busy charting that bright new world, it is good to keep certain things in mind.

Absolute Truth

Certain things cannot be decided upon by your culture. Four will always be twice as big as two and Henry Ford will always be the inventor of the Model T. Absolute truth is that which is always true.

Some people think the only absolutes are scientific, mathematical, or historical. They accept any behavior that their peer group accepts and reject whatever it rejects. Christians recognize that there are also moral absolutes— eternal truths about the meaning of life and the right way to live it. To us, Christ's Sermon on the Mount over two thousand years ago is just as relevant to our daily lives as if it had happened yesterday.

The Divine Plan laid out at Creation took into account all eventualities such as nuclear weapons, space flight, and the information age. While our tools have changed, the hands that control them are very like those of Abraham and Moses, and the standards of human decency and the worth of the human being are exactly the same today as they were when Moses came down Mount Sinai to reveal God's law to the Hebrews. God knew—and still knows—how we should live.

In 1859, an American census taker counted a man of color as half a man. By 1869 the law said a man should be counted as a whole man regardless of the color of his skin.

In that case, our attitudes gradually came into line with God's eternal truth. In some cases, our attitudes are drifting away. The important thing to understand is that eternal truths do not drift toward or away from us; they stand as unmoving as it is unchanging. That makes them signposts that show us where we are and where we need to be.

Make no mistake about it: someday we will have to account for our behavior before God as individuals rather than members of a nation or a culture. That is particularly true about our views on marriage, family, and the sanctity of human life.

Relative Truth

Circumstances in the world around you change, just as you change. Houses are no longer lit by gas, trains are not powered by steam, and women are not kept from voting. You can no longer arrive at an airport minutes before your flight takes off and make a mad dash for the gate. You are more likely to search the web than visit the library.

On the other hand, just because something is new does not automatically mean it is better. Despite a lot of wild claims, electric shocks did not cure a wide variety of diseases.

There is always a next big thing, "new and improved," whether it is medical, moral, or political in nature. Some of these things live up to their promises; many others do not. Arm yourself with critical thinking skills, information, and common sense. Sort out the gold from the sand, and hold on to what is truly important.

> **Certain things cannot be decided upon by your culture. Absolute truth is that which is always true.**

Rights and Responsibilities

For every right, there is an equal responsibility. You can turn the phrase around and it is still true: for every responsibility, there is also a right. Some people do not understand how this works, and they are quick to demand their rights while not living up to their responsibilities.

While American liberty allows us to enjoy our human rights, it did not create them any more than it created our bodies or our souls. The God that created you gave you your rights, and His Divine Bill of Rights is found in a most unlikely place—the Ten Commandments (Exodus, Chapter 20). These are not simply random rules-they were given by God to protect us from others and from ourselves.

Note: These statements of faith may be numbered and worded differently by different church traditions, but that does not change their meaning.

I – Place your faith in God alone – God, who gave you life and salvation, satisfies all your truest needs and deepest longings. We should never let any object or idea, wealth, power, or fame act as a substitute god. These false gods will not help you; they will harm you.

II – Worship God alone – Though you may not always feel the presence of God, He is never far away and stands ready to comfort you and hear your prayers. You should not turn to other sources for the comfort that can only come from God, whether they are songs, games, celebrities, social networks, or political figures. Love one another as God has loved you, but do not place human beings on a throne that belongs to God alone. Material goods are intended to help you further God's will for yourself and oth-

ers, but they are powerless to impart salvation. Since the word "worship" comes from "worthship," we must be mindful of the important boundary between being a fan and being a follower.

III – Revere the name of God - A good name, a flag, a monument—anything that symbolizes something noble, pure or just—deserves respect. God's name deserves the highest respect as a symbol yet also a means of access and an instrument of power. Likewise, God will also not hold blameless the people who drag your good name through the mud, laugh at you

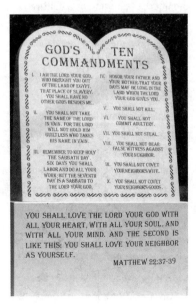

for being religious, or make fun of the wholesome things you do. Language is a gift from God, and you should never use it in ugly or violent ways, or surround yourself with movies, music, or companions who do.

IV – Keep holy the Sabbath - God knows the value of rest. He also knows the importance of setting aside time in our busy schedule to draw near to Him, including regular attendance at church, a strong prayer life, and meaningful service to others. It is common sense to set aside a day of the week to rid yourself of trivial distractions and concentrate on life's highest things.

V - Honor your father and your mother - God understands the importance of family and the central role of parental authority in your future success. He chose to reveal Himself to you as a guiding Father and an obedient Son, as well as the love between them in the form of the Holy Spirit. We should use God's example as a model for our own family lives. In honoring our parents, we should also honor those to whom our parents delegate authority, such as teachers, doctors, and youth leaders.

VI - You shall not murder - God has given you the right to live, just as he gave it to others. Other people do not have the right to kill you, and you don't have the right to kill them. Yet your responsibility goes beyond a passive respect for life. If you truly respect this commandment, you would not stand by the side of the pool and watch someone drown. Such an act would show the same reckless disregard for the value of human life as if you fired a gun in anger.

VII - You shall not commit adultery - God established and blessed the bond between a husband and wife in ways that must not be ignored or compromised. He intended that blessing for you, too, should you ever meet the right person. Purity of mind puts you in a position to receive that blessing. Even now, your purity of mind is a way you can honor the woman you might marry one day.

VIII - You shall not steal – Each of us has stewardship over the material blessings God entrusts to us. Other people should respect your stewardship, and you should respect theirs. You should also recognize cheating to be a form of stealing.

IX - You shall not bear false witness against your neighbor - God created us with a yearning for justice and a need to trust one another. Honesty is the basis of trust and the guide of justice. Truth and justice are gifts from God that we were meant to have and use properly. The consequences of tampering with them or obstructing them involve your relationship with God as well as your standing with other people.

X - You shall not covet - God entrusts to everyone certain talents and opportunities. Your neighbors should appreciate and develop their own blessings rather than envying yours. You should not envy the blessings God gave others, whether it is a new bike or car, parents who are happily married, or the affections of another person. Remember the difference between coveting things and being inspired to develop them for yourself. You may see one of your friends in the troop get the Freedom Award and be inspired to work harder on your own advancement. That is not coveting.

Duties of a Citizen

There are several duties that citizens perform that help make America a better place for all people to live.

Loyalty: Working to make America the best it can be is the ultimate display of loyalty. Some people do this by serving in the armed forces; others do it by working for charities, supporting causes, or holding political office.

Payment of Taxes: You pay for private property like the groceries you use or the clothes you wear. You also pay for public property, such as roads, and public services, such as police and fire protection, through taxation.

Obedience to the Law: Obeying the law is an important duty of citizenship. You may feel justified in ignoring laws you do not like, yet think how you feel when other people choose to ignore laws you do like! There is a democratic process for changing undesirable laws, and you should make your voice be heard at elections, referendums, and town meetings.

Always remember that God's law is the highest law of all.

Cooperation With Public Officials: During an emergency, fire trucks, police cars, and ambulances do not have time to wait for you. It is the legal and moral duty of a citizen to give them the right-of-way. It is also your duty to obey legal orders given you by public officials and to cooperate with law enforcement to reduce crime.

Gainful Employment: As you have the opportunity and ability, you should contribute more to the world than you take from it. This strengthens the economy, builds your character, and sets a good example for others.

Jury Duty: Because Americans have a right to a trial by jury, the justice system is in need of citizens of good character to listen to court trials and decide if someone is guilty or innocent. You should be willing to serve if called.

Participation in Elections: Casting a ballot is not only a right, it is a responsibility. You should learn what you can about the candidates and the issues that affect you and vote according to your conscience.

Public Spirit: There are duties we perform that are not listed in the laws of the United States. When we give gifts of money in church or contribute to causes we believe in, we help make America a better place. Even little gestures of basic human kindness, like washing our hands when we prepare food to keep down the spread of disease, are ways we keep America strong. They are not required by man's law, but they certainly fall under the Golden Rule.

THE UNITED STATES FLAG

The United States Flag is a symbol of our country, but it is also a unique and beautiful picture of an idea you cannot see or touch.

The blue canon of the flag is a sky in which fifty stars shine in a constellation representing the fifty states (a constellation is a pattern of stars that seem to form a picture). The constellation on the American flag stands for a country where all states are equally important, so all of the stars are the same size and equally spaced.

By federal law there is not one particular star that represents your state; they are all to be taken as a whole. Think of that next time you recite the Pledge of Allegiance and say the words, "One nation under God, indivisible..."

Even during the American Civil War when some states left the Union to form a separate Confederacy, the number of stars on the United States Flag was not reduced.

The thirteen stripes in red and white represent the thirteen original states that fought Great Britain for their independence.

Hoisting and Lowering the Flag

To raise the flag, attach it to the halyard (rope) carefully with the help of an assistant so that it is not allowed to touch the ground, then hoist it briskly and respectfully to the top of the flagpole and tie it off.

Lower the flag slowly and respectfully, retrieving it from the halyard with the help of an assistant who keeps it from touching the ground. This gives the act of lowering the flag a certain dignity and helps you avoid the appearance

of being anxious to pull down the symbol of our country in a hurry.

Folding the Flag

Holding the flag waist high between yourself and your assistant, fold the flag in half lengthwise twice. Keep the canon (stars) on the outside. While you hold the flag by the canon, your assistant should make a triangular fold in his end. Continue folding the flag in triangles until only the canon is visible.

The Flag at Half-Staff

On appropriate days of mourning, the flag is hoisted rapidly to the top of the flagpole as detailed above in "Hoisting the Flag." The flag is then lowered slowly and respectfully halfway down the pole and tied off. The flag is retrieved by hoisting it from half-staff to the top rapidly before lowering it slowly in the usual manner. Unless the flag is at half-staff (sometimes called half-mast), it should be hoisted to the very top of the flagpole.

THE HIGHEST CITIZENSHIP

While you seek to be a good citizen of your family, your town, your country, and your world, you should also seek to be a child of God and a citizen of His Kingdom. Your freedom as a United States citizen leaves you at the trailhead to Heaven, but from there you have to choose one of many paths that split off in different directions.

Some people believe all paths are equal, but always remember that only one leads to Jesus Christ and the joy and life He intends you to have. When you come face to face with God it will not be as an American but as a man, and your record must speak for itself without any constitutional protections or Supreme Court rulings. Resolve today—this very minute—to walk worthy, and live a life that speaks well of you as a man. If you do, you'll automatically be a great American.

Being a good citizen of God's Kingdom takes a lifetime to master, but that's exactly what you have—a lifetime! And you have your troop and church friends pulling for you at every step.

Pulling Together

You were created in the image of a Triune God: a Father, Son, and Holy Spirit. While it is helpful to worship God in private at times, feeling close to Him on a lonely mountain top or a quiet forest glade, it is also important for you to be a good citizen of your family and of the body of Christ.

Connecting with your church and your family completes you in ways that you cannot feel while sitting alone in a corner. In the greater sense, you are never truly alone since God is with you always, yet God understands your need to have friends you can see and touch.

> **Resolve today—this very minute—to walk worthy, and live a life that speaks well of you as a man.**

Accountability

We all hate to be nagged. Being told to clean your room and make up your bed day after day gets old fast, especially when it is followed by, "How many times do I have to tell you?"

Yet even you have to admit that certain promises we make are easier to keep if at least one other person knows about them. There are a lot of really dumb things we are careful not to do in front of other people. That's called accountability, and it's a great thing to have when we know what's right and need a little help keeping us on track.

The people most likely to help you form and achieve worthwhile goals are those who share your values and your faith in God.

Standards

Many things in the world around you have standards. For the Christian the Bible is our standard. Not everything that comes out

> Many things in the world around you have standards. For the Christian the Bible is our standard. Not everything that comes out of an oil well is gasoline, and not everything that comes out of a lake is drinking water. If you want to be considered a Christian, your belief in Jesus should affect the things you do, think, and say.

of an oil well is gasoline, and not everything that comes out of a lake is drinking water. If you want to be considered a Christian, your belief in Jesus should affect the things you do, think, and say.

Freedom of speech is a won-

derful right for which many brave men fought and died. They did not die for our right to use profanity. Freedom of speech is about the free expression of ideas, and every idea that can be expressed can be communicated clearly and forcefully without the use of vulgar words.

When you give your word, you should take every reasonable step to keep it. To be trusted and believed under all circumstances is a wonderful thing. Get caught in a lie about one thing, and everything else you say will be picked apart to see if you really meant it.

Remember how good it felt to give your Mom or Dad a gift that was something he or she really wanted? Common courtesy is just another way of saying you give the gifts of patience, respect, and kindness to the people you meet each day. It's not just the right thing to do; it feels good. With practice, you'll get to where you feel uncomfortable being rude to people. That's when you know you're a true gentleman.

You can take action or you can just react. Reactors are people who constantly react to what is going on around them. If it is raining, they are gloomy. If something is irksome, they gripe. Anyone with a pulse can be a reactor. People who take action decide how they will be. If it is raining, they can be cheerful and make other people cheerful, too. If it is uncomfortable, they can have a sense of humor about it. If there is danger, they think of others and maintain their calm as best they can while thinking of something constructive to do. Trailmen try to be actors, not reactors.

Some people will tell you that anything that does not hurt other people is okay. When you refuse alcohol, tobacco, or drugs they may make fun of you or accuse you

of being judgmental. They don't understand that in lowering your own personal standards, you are actually hurting other people who love you and admire you. You are a part of God's Kingdom, and whatever you do to hurt yourself hurts the Kingdom. It also hurts your family and your true friends—friends who want what's best for you. Resolve today to keep your standards high and your life on track.

Whenever people are **well-informed**, they can be **trusted** with their own government.

—*Thomas Jefferson*

3

YOUR HERITAGE

America is a nation that was shaped by frontiers of many kinds: frontiers of wilderness, ideas, and technology. The opportunities presented by a new world drew the ambitious, the adventurous, and the idealistic to give up the comfort of a long-established civilization and create a new social order across the sea.

A NEW LAND

Educated people believed that the world was round long before 1492. However, most of them believed the world was much smaller. The first explorers to cross the Atlantic thought they could go directly from Europe to China. That is why some islands in the Caribbean were called the "West Indies" and the native North Americans were called "Indians." These lands were mistaken for India.

When it was first known that these were new lands, it started a rush of settlers, prospectors, and adventurers who were interested in owning property and what may lie beneath it or live upon it. Nations like England, France, and Spain had the resources to start colonies and the naval might to protect them; these nations claimed large portions of what would become the United States. They opened these lands to people who would make a return on their financial and military investment. These lands were not new to everyone. After all, there had been people in the Americas long before the coming of European explorers. Once it became certain the Americas were new continents and that the local peoples were not actually Indian or Chinese, Europeans were faced with a culture that was never mentioned in the Bible. This confusion led some explorers to wonder if Native Americans were truly human.

Fortunately, enlightened forces in the Christian church soon laid the question of humanity to rest. From our modern perspective, the idea of claiming inhabited lands for a foreign power may strike us as selfish or downright criminal, but we must remember that these Europeans did not consider tribes a legitimate form of national government. They saw themselves as bringing order out of anarchy and realized that if they did not make claims of their own, others would do so. This question of who controlled what also had ominous military significance, since an enemy nation controlling the West Atlantic would be catastrophic. The ability to repair and provision ships on both sides of the ocean, added to income from mining, timber harvesting, trapping, and farming, would give any one nation a terrible advantage over all others.

> **The struggle for religious freedom would ultimately define America and give it the sense of purpose it needed.**

Given that so much was at stake militarily and economically in controlling this new world, it might seem odd that America would ever become a leader in the pursuit of freedom and human rights. Yet the Christian faith that came with the settlers held the seeds of this transformation within it. It was the idea that spiritual security was more important than naval bases, gold mines, or lumber mills. The struggle for religious freedom would ultimately define America and give it the sense of purpose it needed. It is this America—the land of freedom—that you are most familiar with and for which so many fought and died.

NEW IDEAS

To get enough people to settle these new colonies, these settlers in the New World were willing to be more tolerant of differing points of view on religion and social order. The atmosphere of freedom drew a number of people who otherwise were not very adventurous and cared little for rumors of gold and jewels. These people wanted the freedom to lay up their treasures in Heaven, and they were not disappointed. The most famous of these groups were the Puritans of Massachu-

setts, the Quakers of Pennsylvania, the Anabaptists of Rhode Island, and the Catholics of Maryland.

Even in America, however, some old ideas died hard. Only after a costly and tragic Civil War did the United States outlaw slavery in 1865. Women were not allowed to vote until 1920. The right of every child to attend the public school of his or her choice has only been guaranteed since 1968. No doubt the struggle to define the boundaries of freedom will continue during your lifetime, even as it will for your children. As a Christian, it is your responsibility to set these boundaries with wisdom and faithfulness. After all, freedom and human rights are not human inventions. They came from God in the beginning of all things, and it is our right—and responsibility—to discover their full extent and to enable them to be enjoyed safely and openly.

NEW TECHNOLOGIES

Before the United States had celebrated its hundredth birthday, it saw a number of enormously important technological advances that changed the way people lived,

thought, and communicated.

Water power ran busy factories where machines did the work of a hundred men. This advance made goods cheaper, but it also lowered wages.

The steam locomotive brought far-flung places within the reach of ordinary people. America was a huge place with great centers of learning, farming, and industry separated by hundreds of miles. Railroads brought them closer together at a price the average person could afford, making them the jet airplanes of their day.

The telegraph made it possible for President Lincoln to send orders from Washington DC to Union Generals fighting in distant battlefields

of the Civil War and get same-day reports of the results. When Lincoln was assassinated, people read about it in their newspapers the same day. It was the humble beginnings of today's information age.

Ships were no longer at the mercy of the wind. With paddle-

wheel engines powered by steam, boats could go upriver as easily as they went downriver. Before this invention, it was cheaper to build a new barge to take goods down the Mississippi River and sell it for lumber in New Orleans than it was to make a round trip.

NEW RESPONSIBILITIES

America became a single nation in 1776. However, it was not until after the American Civil War that the rest of the world viewed the United States as a major world power.

George Washington had warned those American presidents who would follow him to "avoid entangling foreign alliances." This started many years of a policy known as "isolationism" in which America distanced itself from much of European political wrangling and kept to itself behind the moats of the Atlantic and Pacific Oceans.

Two World Wars taught the United States that it was very much a part of the rest of the world and could no longer afford to ignore global politics. After the Japanese attack on Pearl Harbor in 1941, it became clear to all Americans that if the United States did not go to the world, the world would come to the United States.

By the time the Second World War ended in 1945, America emerged as a giant on the world stage with its fleet of aircraft carriers and the first atomic bombs. It also carried its share of responsibility for the prevention of future world wars.

NEW HORIZONS

We live in an age of great challenges and great promise. Just as American boys born in 1925 never dreamed they would be fighting Nazis, there is only so much we can say for sure about the future you will live in. This much stands firm: that the ideals that made America great can live on inside you, and you have as much a chance of making a difference in the world as those who came before.

NEW STEWARDSHIP

The Trailman's Oath acknowledges our duty to, "...be a good steward of creation." We never truly own anything. It is merely entrusted to us for our lifetime and we pass things on as a legacy to future generations.

It is important that we preserve the liberties that were handed down to us by our forbearers, keep the water and air clean and the forests and wildlife plentiful. It is important that we set a good example and show respect for all the great ideals we want our children to uphold. After all, God created this world. We see Him when we see the sand of the sea, the number of the waves; the wonder of rain drops and snowflakes, the majesty of mountains, and the beautiful canopy of stars – too numerous to count. Let all creation remind you of the Creator. Always view the world as a work of art, displayed for our admiration. We are called to be stewards of the beauty of our world. God's will is for the world to continue to bring forth food in abundance, at the proper seasons, for humans and animals and everything that lives on it. The great Creator and Lord of the universe has created this world to exist in peace and harmony for our enjoyment and our health. God provides all that we need, but it is up to us to respect and maintain it.

This kind of stewardship requires courage and self-discipline. When Jesus commanded us to do unto our neighbors as we would want done unto ourselves, he also referred to neighbors not yet born!

4

RELATIONSHIPS

YOUR RELATIONSHIP WITH GOD

Throughout life you will form many relationships, and some of them will be very important to you. The most important relationship you will ever have is with your Heavenly Father. God is a living, personal being, and He wants to have a close and meaningful relationship with you as His child. One of the ways you build that relationship is through prayer. The leaders in your troop and church can help you improve your prayer life and deepen your relationship with God as you follow Jesus. Rely upon their guidance, and bring them your questions about God and the Christian faith.

Trail Life USA is designed to closely resemble your journey in life: the trail represents the path you walk as you search for adventure and as you seek to follow Christ. The most important course you will set on your journey is to follow Jesus along the straight and narrow path.

If you don't yet have Christ in your life, you have a hole in your heart and mind that only He can fill. If you are not able to talk with a pastor, a parent, or a troop leader about God then you can start praying like this:

"Dear Lord Jesus, I know I am a sinner, and I ask your forgiveness. I believe You died for my sins and rose from the dead showing that You were God. I trust and follow You as my Lord and Savior. Guide me and help me to do Your will. In your name, amen."

Making this commitment is a major step in the right direction along the trail of life. When you make this decision you should follow up by contacting someone you trust and respect in your family, your church, or your Troop and see where you should go from there.

RELATIONSHIPS WITH FAMILY

A family is a group of persons that is related to each other by the ties of marriage, blood, or adoption. Families come in many shapes and sizes. You may have brothers or sisters, older siblings or younger ones, or you may be an only child.

You may have your birth parents, or you may be missing one or both parents. You may even be adopted. Try to be grateful for what you have and choose not to envy others.

Some people are quite happy with the way things are in their family, while others may be very unhappy or even angry. If you are like most people, you fall somewhere between those extremes. Just precisely where you stand depends on you. Just as you have some control over how you handle rain on a campout, you have a certain amount of control over how happy your family is by the way you react to circumstances. You have much more control over your attitude than you do over your luck;

so work on your attitude now while you wait for your luck to improve.

Family relationships are quite different from friendships. You can pick or choose your friends, but—like it or not—you cannot pick and choose your family. You would do well to treat your family relationships with great care: the lingering bitterness of a strained relationship with a brother or parent will haunt you far longer than a breakup with a high school buddy.

Relationships are not always easy. You may be upset if you have to work harder around the house because of the loss of a parent or the presence of younger children around the house. Your friends at school may have more free time because they have fewer chores and you feel this is unfair. You may be upset if you don't get the same privileges and freedom as an older brother or sister, and the fact they were under more restrictions when they were your age does not make it easier to bear. You may think that your parents love a brother or sister more than they love you. These difficult feelings are common for kids to have and you need to deal with

them, but that does not mean they are true. Facing these challenges with determination, patience, and a sense of humor is a good sign that you are becoming a man.

It may be helpful for you to remember families in the Bible. Even the people God chose to lead great campaigns and start great nations had their troubles. Think about Joseph in the Old Testament whose brothers nearly killed him. They sold him into slavery and told his father Joseph had been killed. Over the years Joseph came to forgive his brothers, and when he had risen to a position of great power, he chose to forgive their crime rather than punish them.

You can learn two things from this story; first, that God expects a lot from you when he says to love your enemies, and second, forgiving others is the real path to freedom and spiritual prosperity. Some families have been split because of a dispute, an offense or a really bad argument, and they never again speak to each other. This prevents us from living free and loving the way God wants us to love—even

> **Facing these challenges with determination, patience, and a sense of humor is a good sign that you are becoming a man.**

our enemies. Family conflicts can be some of the most difficult in our life. But we must learn to humble ourselves and ask God and others for forgiveness. It is unlikely Joseph would have prospered and then went on to great positions of influence if he had spent his whole life hating his brothers. Humility and forgive-

> Humility and forgiveness are two of the great secrets to spiritual success in the Christian life. The Trailman who finds and uses these tools will go far in life.

ness are two of the great secrets to spiritual success in the Christian life. The Trailman who finds and uses these tools will go far in life.

As you mature, your relationship with your parents will change. You will be given new rights and new responsibilities that reflect less and less the boy you were and more and more the man you are becoming. It is natural for you to feel pride in your newfound abilities, and it is also natural that you will start questioning some decisions your parents make. At times it will feel like they are treating you like a younger child, and that can be frustrating. You may be tempted at

times to forget your special relationship with your parents and treat them the way you might treat other people. In many ways they **are** like other people. They make mistakes and they may even have bad habits. That said, unless they ask you to do something that violates the laws of God or man, you should respect their parental authority. This is part of your duty to respect authority which is found in the Trailman Oath. That extends as well to the people that your parents delegate to have authority over you, such as teachers, doctors, clergy, and Troop leaders. Respecting parental authority does not mean you cannot express your side of an issue. If you raise objections in a respectful manner, especially if you explain your line of reasoning, you will come to see they respect your thoughts and feelings even if they don't always come to agree with them.

The fifth of the Ten Commandments in the Bible is to "Honor your Father and Mother" and it is the first commandment with a promise. That promise is that we will live a long life! A very big part of honor is respect.

Younger siblings can try your patience. Even so, you are more of a role model to them than they may think. They pick up your habits and imitate your manners. In the Trailman Oath we also repeat the words "treat others they way we would like to be treated." You should always treat your brothers and sisters the way you want your parents to treat you. You may find that things you learn about leadership in your troop also work quite well in your family—whether it is giving guidance with the right attitude, or receiving it likewise.

RELATIONSHIPS WITH FRIENDS

Friends are some of your greatest treasures. There are many people who recognize you and treat you well, but only some of them are true friends. So how do you know if you are truly a friend to someone, or they are a real friend to you? Friends want what is best for each other—even if that means talking you out of making a bad decision. They are always willing to help; you don't have to beg a close friend for a favor—as long as what you are asking for is not harmful and is consistent with our duties to our God, family, country, and community. A true friend is loyal and stands up for you and defends you—and you do the same for them. Friends are

happy and rejoice in your successes and achievements, and are also there for you when things aren't going so well. Friends appreciate and like you for who you are. It has been said that a true friend is a person that knows *everything* about you ... and is still your friend.

If you are lucky enough to have such good friends, make sure you are a good friend back to them. When they need to complain, or

> If you are lucky enough to have such good friends, make sure you are a good friend back to them. The best way to have good friends is to be one.

they are scared or upset, you should listen to them and offer encouragement and help. If you don't have friends like that yet, remember this time-tested advice: the best way to **have** good friends is to **be** one.

RELATIONSHIPS WITH NEIGHBORS

Neighbors are special people who are not our family but live closer to us than the rest of the people in the world. Neighbors are important because the closer a person lives

to you the greater your duty is to care for them and help them. Our first duty is to those actually living with us, usually our family. But our next duty is to our neighbors. Jesus said to love your neighbor. When families in neighborhoods help each other then our communities, our state, and our whole country becomes stronger. Have you ever helped an older neighbor with an outdoor chore? Has your family ever brought a meal over to a neighboring mother who just had a baby? Have you ever offered to help organize a neighborhood garage sale? Have your parents ever agreed to care for a neighbor's pet while they were out of town? These are all ways we can become good neighbors. Can you think of a way you can be a good neighbor? Always get your parents' permission before you talk to or work with neighbors.

RELATIONSHIPS WITH STRANGERS

There are so many people in the world. We should be friendly and show Christian concern for all people not just those we know in our family and among neighbors.

Imagine you are in an airplane. Night has fallen and out your window you see tiny yellow dots below you like stars in the sky. Those dots are people going about their lives. While you may never see them again, they are made as fully in the image of God as your schoolmates, your parents, your friends, the woman you may marry someday, and the children you may one day bring into the world. Some Christian missionaries even devote their whole lives to help and reach people in foreign countries whom they have never met.

The great American humorist Will Rogers once said that strangers are friends you have not met. While your mind and heart may limit the number of deep friendships you can maintain, you should show all people the same consideration and courtesy you would your own family and friends, just as you would want them to show kindness to you and to those you love. As Jesus said, "Love one another as I have loved you."

RELATIONSHIPS AND RISK

On one hand we should be concerned with friends, neighbors and even strangers, but on the other hand, some neighbors or strangers can be risky or even dangerous. Therefore, you should always rely on your parent's advice and permission when talking with or doing any activity with people outside your family

Managing relationships is an art you can master, and the best relationships take time and effort. Mastering relationships is hard, but worthwhile. Even good hearts have their share of spills. That's normal, and with time and some help you will regain confidence and reach out again.

Friendships are like wheels. You are the hub and your relationships are the spokes. The challenge is that the spokes not only meet at the hub, they are also connected to each other around the rim. The people you care about may know one another, and their relationships may range from deep love all the way to blatant hostility. You may even find yourself caught in the middle of an argument between two of your friends, with each one expecting you to take sides—that is never a good place to be. Tell them that being asked to take sides is an unfair imposition on your friendship and, if you are lucky, it will end there.

Sometimes you may not be so lucky. Dylan's parents fought a lot about their finances and hurt feelings. They would say ugly things that often turned to threats. One day after an especially bad fight, Dad packed his suitcase and went to live in a hotel. Dylan thought that was the worst thing that could happen to them, but things got even worse. At the divorce hearing, the judge asked Dylan if he would rather live with Mom or Dad. Both of his parents were looking at him intently as he took in a breath, let it out slowly, and said, "Mom." His father looked away, head bowed and hands knotting into fists, and this made Dylan want to curl up and die.

At this point Dylan had two choices; he could choose to seek comfort in his friends and his faith, or he could protect his vulnerable heart from being hurt again by withdrawing from friendships and blaming God and himself for letting this happen.

Fortunately for Dylan, his pastor had a talk with him. He learned that the divorce was not his fault and that he did not cause the money problems and neglect that drove his parents apart. Dylan took the best possible course of action: he learned from his parents' mistakes and asked God to help him avoid making the same mistakes with his own wife and children.

DANGEROUS RELATIONSHIPS

You try to choose friends who truly like you and build you up, and to avoid people who merely use you and drag you down. Still there are times when someone gains your trust and love as a way to get what they want. It may be something small and harmless like a favor. We all have "friends" who only look us up when they want us to do them a favor. Some people want bigger things that can get you in bad trouble, steal your innocence, or threaten your very safety. There are not many of these people, but even one in your life is too much.

Sometimes parents may not be happy with your choice of friends. Parents may not understand why you like a person whom they dislike or that causes them concern. It can leave you with a sense of being caught in the middle. If this happens, talk with your parents so that they can understand why you like the person, and so you can understand why they do not like them. We are all called by God to honor our parents. Communicating honestly and with a true spirit of understanding and compassion is what God calls us to do.

Ethan had an Uncle Bob who was smart and funny, and always bought him the nicest presents. Ethan's mother invited Bob over very often because she was a widow and Bob was a good male role model for her son. When Bob took Ethan to see football games or visit the zoo the way his father used to do, Ethan felt good inside. One day while they were boating alone on the lake, Bob took out his smartphone and asked Ethan if he would like to see some pictures of people with no clothes. Ethan was shocked by what he saw.

"I don't think I should be looking at those," Ethan said, because he had been told about inappropriate things on the Internet. So Bob put the phone away and did not mention it again. When Ethan got home, he wondered if he should tell his mother what happened, but he was afraid to say anything. After all, Bob was her brother and the whole thing was embarrassing.

> Sometimes even people that we trust do things that are wrong, and can intend to misuse our trust and hurt us. Any act that threatens to harm your physical, mental, emotional, or spiritual health is wrong.

Finally Ethan had to say something. His mother was upset, but she knew her son would not lie to her. She reported the incident to the authorities. It turns out that the photos on the phone were of children who were being abused. Bob was made to get the help he needed and the pictures led the police to other people who were harming boys like Ethan. It was a good thing he spoke up.

Sometimes even people that we trust do things that are wrong, and can intend to misuse our trust and hurt us. Any act that threatens to harm your physical, mental, emotional, or spiritual health is wrong. Unfortunately, there are some adults or even other youth who sexually abuse children. Any sexual contact with a youth—regardless of who the other person is—is wrong and should be reported. The following guidelines can help to reduce the possibility of that happening to you or other youth:

- Everyone should respect your privacy—especially when it comes to toilets, showering, and sleeping arrangements.

> Your mind and your body are two things over which you have certain rights that other people cannot take away.

- You should never be alone with only one adult (unless it is your parent).
- There should be no secret ceremonies, secret activities, or secret meetings.
- Appropriate clothing should always be worn—especially for swimming activities.
- There should be no hazing, bullying, or physical hitting.
- Cameras, cell phones, and other electronics should never be used inappropriately or in any

way that can violate someone's privacy or cause them any harm.

If anyone fails to follow these guidelines, you should report them to your leaders and to your parents. It is the right thing to do and can help to protect you and others from harm.

Your mind and your body are two things over which you have certain rights that other people cannot take away. A doctor may need to examine you in a very personal and private way, but if it makes you feel uncomfortable tell your parents or ask one of them to be with you during the examination. People may say things to you about ideas with which you don't agree. If people go beyond what you think or have been taught is reasonable, or if they ask you to see, read or do things that make you feel uncomfort- able—whether it's a physical act or a spiritual one—you have the right to refuse, and that is precisely what you should do. If they offer you alcohol, illegal drugs, or ask you to help them steal something, or they touch you or ask you to touch them in inappropriate ways, go find someone you trust and tell them. Tell them more than once if you have to, or tell other trusted adults. If

you can't get through to them, find someone else until you are believed.

How do you know if something is wrong? One of the best things to do is to look for God's direction. It is that gut feeling based on reason, love, and developing your conscience by studying moral issues and the Bible's teaching on them. The more you develop your conscience, the easier it will be to know what the right thing to do is.

Adults should know better than to ask young people to perform sexual acts, disobey the law, or violate their religious principles. It is never your fault if someone asks you to do something wrong, even if they say it is. **Say NO, then GO, and TELL**.

HEALTH & FITNESS

5

FITNESS

In a sense, every Trailman wears two uniforms. The one on the outside can be cleaned when soiled or replaced when it no longer serves you well. The one on the inside is the uniform God gave you (your body) to carry you through life. When this uniform gets damaged it might heal, but it is far better that you take good care of it in the first place so you can keep it attractive and get years of faithful service from it.

FOUR TYPES OF FITNESS

There are four types of fitness common to mankind. **Emotional fitness** does not mean being happy all the time. God gave you a full range of emotions, and there is an appropriate time for each of them, even anger. It is important not to let your feelings run amok and lead you to act in ways that are not appropriate. **Physical fitness** is good stewardship of your body so you can do more things safely and comfortably and enjoy a longer lifespan and more years of independence. **Moral fitness** is the ability to make difficult decisions where what you want and what you need conflict or where you run the risk of being unpopular.

Mental fitness is about getting an education, developing your powers of reason, and learning from your mistakes.

All four types of fitness—mental, moral, physical, and emotional—have certain things in common. They all benefit from a good diet, plenty of exercise, and getting enough rest.

EMOTIONAL FITNESS

Did you ever play a game with a bad loser? It's no fun at all. Either they win and they rub it in, or they lose and they sulk about it.

Did you ever go out on a campout with a "Gloomy Gus?" When it rains or the food is not to his liking,

Gloomy Gus complains endlessly.

These are two irritating examples of poor emotional fitness. Not all people with poor emotional fitness react unpleasantly. Some of them withdraw and keep to themselves. Whether or not their behavior spoils troop morale, it is a wellness problem.

Handling Disappointment

You can be sure that no one likes disappointment. Whether you were not elected First Officer or you did not get that summer job you really wanted, you can either come up with "Plan B" to fill the hole in your life, or you can sulk and feel resentful. Ask yourself which method is most likely to ease your disappointment: a new approach or hurt feelings?

Anger Management

When we see the weak victimized by the strong, we get angry. When we find that people we trust with authority misuse their power, we get angry. These feelings are called righteous indignation, and they are a gift from God that keeps us from tolerating things that are totally unacceptable.

Other things make us angry too, but that sort of anger is not always appropriate. That's the kind of anger you feel when you lose your temper. Perhaps you did not get something you thought you deserved. Perhaps you felt like someone "took" your usual spot or that a bit of advice was "insulting your intelligence."

That sort of anger is not a gift from God; it's more of a challenge to our character. A wise Trailman rises up to meet that challenge and wins.

When you're angry, your body goes into overdrive. You get a burst of energy, and your heartbeat and respiration increase. The best thing is for you to use that energy constructively. Fix the problem by sweeping up the broken glass, stacking up the fallen canned goods, or finding something that had nothing to do with your anger but needs some real "elbow grease" applied. A physically intense task can help work the anger out of your system.

If you can't sweat out that surge of anger, delay your reaction. The physical part of your anger that makes you want to break things subsides very quickly. Your urge to say something really crushing is like a sand castle on the beach when the tide of your common sense comes in; after a few waves wash over it, it flattens out nicely. There is a lot of wisdom in that old custom of counting to ten before responding. Cool off, breathe deeply, and pretend that what you'll say or do will be recorded to watch later with your parents.

Measured responses are best. That's when you judge how strongly you need to react and keep to

that limit. Blurting out something really hurtful or taking a swing at someone who offended you only makes things worse. You may lose a friend forever, and while that may not seem like a great loss while you're still angry, there may come a time when you regret having said things you can't take back.

> When you're angry, your body goes into overdrive. You get a burst of energy, and your heartbeat and respiration increase. The best thing is for you to use that energy constructively.

Stick to the conflict at hand. If you're not making headway during a conflict, don't latch on to some different thing to give you an edge. If you're on a campout and somebody didn't watch the stove and burned your meal, don't bring up that he borrowed your flashlight on the last campout without asking. Such a reaction muddies the matter at hand, making it more difficult to resolve things.

Most importantly, remember not to let the sun go down on your wrath. Real life problems don't always sort themselves out in a half hour the way they do on sitcoms, but you should make a good faith effort not to let things spill over into tomorrow. Think about the case of best friends Jimmy and Billy. Jimmy's family had to move away suddenly, and he went to see Billy to say goodbye. Unfortunately, they got into an argument before Jimmy got around to the point of his visit. Billy made him so angry that he left. Billy came to regret what he had said that started the argument and went to Jimmy's house, only to find it empty. For a long time, Billy thought he would never get to say he was sorry. Luckily, he found Jimmy's family on Facebook and got his chance to make up. Those second chances don't always happen.

> Most importantly, remember not to let the sun go down on your wrath. Real life problems don't always sort themselves out in a half hour the way they do on sitcoms, but you should make a good faith effort not to let things spill over into tomorrow.

Fear and Anxiety

You can bet fear serves a useful purpose. Setting your clothes on fire or jumping out of a window are things you should fear because they are genuinely harmful. Sometimes we get afraid of things that are not real dangers, such as speaking in front of groups or messing up in front of our friends. The good news is that having fear does not make us cowards. Real heroes do not let fear prevent them from doing the right thing. The bad news is that being a real hero does not make the fear any less hurtful. Sometimes you just have to tough it out. But then comes good news again: when it's over, you feel really good about yourself, and that makes it all worthwhile.

Anxiety is being afraid of fear. Johnny was out in the yard playing when he should have been up in his room studying for a test. His father looked out the back door and said, "we need to talk." When Johnny came into the house, his father scolded him and took away his Internet access for a week. Later on, Johnny was playing in the yard, and his father came to the back door and said, "we need to talk." Johnny's mind raced through all the possible things he might have done wrong to make his father angry and all the terrible punishments that might lie ahead. It turned out that the talk was merely a friendly chat about using the Internet safely.

Once something really terrible happens, it leaves a trail behind.

When new experiences bring us within sight of that trail, our minds race toward the disaster that surely must lie ahead. The problem is that this sort of thinking serves no useful purpose. When you feel yourself being snagged by unpleasant associations, find someone you trust and get it out into the open. Sometimes, not being the only one who knows about it is a great step in dealing with it positively.

MENTAL FITNESS

Your mind is like a backpack. The brighter you are, the bigger the backpack—and the more knowledge you can stuff into it! But just because your backpack is big does not mean it will pack itself.

To carry this idea a step further, worthless thoughts are like worthless things. You wouldn't fill your backpack with things you'll never use. You would make sure you put all the important things in first. So while it's alright to be the top video gamer of your Troop, you can be sure killing war-bots is not going to help you get a job as a doctor or an English teacher or make you more comfortable on a campout. Make sure you learn worthwhile things, too.

It may sound odd, but the more you learn, the easier it is to learn. In

Learning How to Learn

There are things you can do to make studying easier:

- Study **at the same time of day**. It helps you get in the proper mood.
- Keep your study area **free of distractions** such as TV, radio, and video games. Having **more than one place** to study actually helps keep your mental focus.
- **Switch subjects** when you feel your mind wandering instead of spending a solid hour reading nothing but history.
- Make sure you **get enough sleep!**
- **Never put off studying** until the night before a test.

a way it's like pushups: with practice, you increase the amount you do at one time, and you develop better form so that you don't waste effort. As you build your knowledge, you will start seeing relationships between new facts and the ones you already know.

You can increase your powers of observation, too. There are people who notice a lot of things about everyone they meet. These people are not necessarily much smarter than you; they just developed the habit of observing things. Sometimes the skill can make all the difference, as when you are reporting an accident.

Learning people's names is especially important. Old friends you have not seen in a while feel good when you recognize them and call them by name. You make a better Patrol Leader when you remember the new guy and confidently call him by name.

> **A Trailman should go for best and not just settle for good**

MORAL FITNESS

Morals need exercise too, and they don't get it when you try to pass difficult decisions to someone else.

But what about resting your morals? You can do that when you delegate responsibility to others. Learning who to trust and how to let go will keep you from burning out. You also give your morals a rest when you take overwhelming problems to your parents or religious leaders for advice.

Do you ever make New Year's resolutions? For a while they are very easy to keep, but then you have to get out of bed on January lst, and the solemn promises you made start to get a little shaky. Yes, some promises feel very good when you're making them, but a promise is like a purchase. When you first put your hands on it, it feels great, but then comes the bill. The bill for keeping a promise is that you have to do something—usually something you don't really enjoy doing. like cutting down on sweets or taking on extra chores. Being able to keep a promise when it ceases to be fun is one measure of moral fitness.

Good, Better, and Best

Your morals are not merely a set of beliefs; they are ways you react to decisions. They are not always decisions of good versus evil but may be choices among good, better, and best. A Trailman should go for best and not just settle for good.

Once, an Arab trader got separated from his caravan. He wandered the desert alone for days, hungry, thirsty, and discouraged. One night he raised his arms to heaven and said, "Lord, I would do anything you ask of me if you would just get me out of here!"

He heard a voice say, "Feel in the sand around you for the small stones. Pick up some of them and take them with you. Tomorrow, you will find a town, and you will be very happy and very sad."

He did as the voice commanded, and, as promised, he did wander into a good-sized town the next morning. Eager to have a room to rent and a decent meal, he regretted having no gold on him. That's when he remembered the stones. In the sunlight he could see priceless rubies, emeralds, and diamonds. He was carrying a king's ransom! Yes, he was very happy, but he was also sad to realize his pockets could have held ten times that much. He would never find his way back across the shifting sands ... the opportunity was gone forever!

Those sands are the passage of time which eventually buries all opportunities in the past. They are gone quicker than we realize! When we have a chance to go to school and better ourselves or to show family and friends the attention and respect they deserve, we often pick up just enough treasures to get by. It seems good enough at the time, but when we look back on what we did and wish we had done better, it's too late. Each day you live costs you a day off your lifespan. Make sure you get full value for it by applying yourself fully.

Resisting Temptation

No discussion of morals would be complete without talking about resisting temptation.

There is a time and a place for everything. Some people do a very funny stand-up comedy routine that brings joy and laughter to others, but they shouldn't do it at Grandma's funeral!

Every desire a man feels, in its most basic and pure form, is a part of how God made you and is there for a reason. The trick to living a good and fulfilling life is in expressing those desires in normal ways at the right time and under the right circumstances.

There is a time and a place for a healthy adult man to fall in love and want to be close to a woman in a very special kind of way. That place, instituted by God, is called marriage. Sex is a beautiful and needful thing in the right place and time. Sex outside of marriage is not part of God's plan for you. Sexual impurity such as looking at so-called "adult" pictures in magazines, on television or on the Internet pulls you even further from God's plan for you. It complicates life for you as a husband later on as you cannot help but compare your relationship with your wife to casual relationships you've had with other women and things you saw in movies, books, online, or in magazines. Those thoughts are troubling, often raise unrealistic expectations, and do not belong in your happy home. Marriage and family life are wonderful things, and you want yours to be wonderful, too.

Surround yourself only with genuine, worthwhile things. The illusion of pleasure and joy you get from drugs and alcohol is an empty promise that leaves you flat and looking for a way to get the illusion back. It is better you do not go down that road in the first place, but if you have, decide today—this very moment—to quit while you're ahead. Find pleasure and joy in something real that does not destroy you or the people that love and depend on you.

It's nice to have new things. Even a crow likes to collect shiny objects.

> **Find pleasure and joy in something real that does not destroy you or the people that love and depend on you.**

Hard Decisions

Nobody likes to make choices where either outcome is gloomy. While we have a natural tendency to seek the acceptance of others and to please them, our duty sometimes points us in the opposite direction.

If you love someone, you will tell the truth even when he or she wants to hear a lie. You will give advice that only a true friend would give, saying what he or she needs to hear rather than what he or she wants to hear.

Sometimes there are two things you want very badly, and neither one is necessarily a bad thing, but you can't have both. It's at times like that you must remember your priorities: people over goods, family over power, long-term plans over short-term gains.

Whether you realize it or not, every decision you make has its price. The knack of being happy and having self-respect is in getting what's truly important for the right price. After all, no man ever lay on his deathbed wishing he'd spent more time at the office.

It becomes a problem when we make possessions more important than the people who love us and rely on us. It's also wrong to take things we did not earn ourselves. Something you steal or cheat to obtain will never give you the same feeling of pride of ownership as something you earned yourself. Remember that stealing and envy (wanting something in the wrong way) are warned about in two of the Ten Commandments. God must feel very strongly about that for it to make two of his top ten rules.

The best way to resist temptation is to have the right sort of friends. Someone who wants you to lower your moral standards as the price of acceptance is NOT your friend. People who admire you for doing the right thing at the right time and in the right way are true friends.

Of course, you may have done some things that you are ashamed of—perhaps some of the very things mentioned here. The dirt you have on the outside comes off easily with soap and water. Becoming clean in your heart and mind requires scrubbing with the soap of God's grace through Christ Jesus.

PHYSICAL FITNESS

Albert Einstein was a very brilliant man, but he only saw the body as a mechanism to carry the brain around. It is hard to have good thoughts and emotions while your body is rebelling against you with pain and weakness!

You need a healthy body to enjoy the opportunities this world gives you, and if you get off that couch and get active, that's a great first step. Couple that activity with a healthy diet, plenty of rest, and good hygiene, and each day of your life will be an adventure.

Exercise

You can cram for an exam, but exercise is one skill that must be pursued over time. Your body has a budget, just like your household. As your body is exercised over time, the repeated demands your muscles make for energy will result in positive changes to your body. Those changes cannot be requested—or delivered—overnight. You may feel discomfort when you first become serious about exercise. That's a signal to you that the change in your lifestyle is long overdue.

Diet

A well-balanced diet gives you the raw materials to build and repair your body and lots of energy to keep it active. There are a large number of vitamin and mineral supplements you can buy, but that is no substitute for nutritious fare.

There are some things you want to avoid. Too much caffeine and sugar is bad for you, as is a high-fat, high-cholesterol diet. Fast foods are a convenience item, and dessert is a treat for after a regular meal. Neither fast food nor dessert food was meant as an ongoing source of nutrition.

"Energy supplements" that come in a can (like soft drinks) or small bottles are not recommended. A Trailman should steer clear of such things in favor of a proper regimen of exercise, diet, and rest.

Water

You need at least six to eight glasses of fresh water every day.

Water makes up almost three fourths of your body. It does several jobs in the body such as nutrient distribution, waste elimination, and evaporative cooling, which is especially critical during hot weather or strenuous physical activity.

Your Ideal Weight

Your recommended weight is determined by your height and build. Obviously, a healthy 17-year-old should weigh more than a healthy 12-year-old!

Far too many people in America are heavier than they should be. The rate of childhood obesity has tripled since 1980. Extra weight means added health risks, but it also makes the physical activities you enjoy most a lot more strenuous.

To find your ideal weight, search the web for "health calculators," or visit http://www.healthstatus.com/calculate/ideal-weight-children.

Sleep

Sleep is a time when the body can refresh itself and carry out some of its self-repair and growth activities. Most growing boys need at least nine hours

of sleep a night. Adults get by on eight hours, by and large. Of course, not everyone is alike; some people need more sleep than others.

Falling asleep and getting the most restful sleep works best when you go to bed and wake up at the same time every day. Other things besides varying your schedule can spoil a night's sleep. Watching an intense movie (it does not have to be scary) or strenuous activity right before bedtime can delay you from falling asleep. Too many fluids within an hour of heading to bed can wake you at odd hours of the night

> Falling asleep and getting the most restful sleep works best when you go to bed and wake up at the same time every day.

or early morning. A chilly midnight latrine run in late autumn through dewy grass is no fun, and when you return to bed, it's hard to take up your night's sleep where you left off.

AVOIDING DISEASE

As a whole, a Trailman does not mind sharing things, but disease germs should not be shared. Clean all eating utensils well, store food properly, cook food thoroughly, and wash your hands often, especially when you visit the bathroom. Take advantage of sanitizing wipes.

Be sure to get the shots you need. Nobody likes needles, but a momentary stick is nothing like as bad as a severe case of the flu. Some diseases, like tetanus, can kill you.

AVOIDING INJURY

Wear protective gear when you bike, skate, or engage in strenuous activities. Follow safety rules regarding woods tools, knives, and equipment. Wear a personal flotation device while boating or water-skiing. Make absolutely sure you have the right training for potentially dangerous activities so you do not take unnecessary chances and so you will know how to react if faced with the unexpected.

When lifting heavy objects, don't lean over to pick them up. Bend your knees and keep your back straight. Your legs will provide the lift you need.

Use common sense around the house or the campsite. Be aware at all times of branches, hanging pots, or other places where you could bang your head or trip.

TOBACCO, ALCOHOL, AND DRUGS

There are worse things you can put in your body than junk food. Some people abuse tobacco, alcohol, or illegal drugs. These substances are dangerous and habit-forming and should be avoided.

The temporary euphoria people feel while on alcohol or drugs is empty. They are soon left flat and find themselves looking to hide themselves away once more in that illusion of happiness.

Drugs and alcohol impair judgment. In addition to the damage you may do to your body, your lack of control makes you a hazard to yourself and others. Many people die each year from driving under the influence of alcohol or drugs. Many innocent people are struck and killed by people who drive while impaired.

Some people have habits. They may have a habit of putting on the left shoe before the right shoe or of watching certain shows. Other times, it is habits that have people. When craving for tobacco, alcohol, or drugs sets in, you may find yourself changing appointments, giving up certain activities you used to enjoy, or spending excessive amounts of money to get your next dose, your next puff, or your next glass. That's when you know the habit has you, and quitting is very difficult to do without professional help.

It is much better not to put yourself in that position than to have to go through the expense and discomfort of getting rid of a habit that controls your behavior. However, if you have a problem with addiction, do something about it right away.

BULLYING AND HARASSMENT

Some boys love to swim; others love to hike. Those kinds of people are fun to be with. Sadly, there are some boys who enjoy threatening or hurting others. We dread having them around us.

Since bullies get their satisfaction from seeing your reactions, your attempts to avoid them or ignore them may make them try even harder. You may feel trapped. It may even make life seem not worth living.

Bullying is very serious. You may have been told that it is part of becoming a man to face it alone. Why would God expect boys to endure violence alone as part of becoming men? He doesn't! If you tell adults you trust what is happening to you and then begin ignoring the bullying, the bully will either back off or someone in authority will intervene to make the bullying stop. You can even stop someone else from being bullied by telling an adult. When you stop a bully you not only spare yourself a lot of unnecessary grief, you can also help other victims and possibly even the bully himself.

THE BIGGER PICTURE

You are not the only one who benefits from your personal fitness. There are many people who rely on you for the happiness you give them and the skills and knowledge you possess, just as there are many people you need and count on. That makes your personal fitness a part of the wellness of others, just as other peoples' fitness becomes part of your own wellness.

You must learn to think of being healthy as a responsibility you bear. Imagine the surprise of an Army recruit who forgot to use his sunscreen and got badly sunburned. When he showed up in sick bay, he was fined for damaging United States property! You can believe he always used his sunscreen after that.

Be sure to remember that the fitness you owe other people is in all four types: physical, mental, emotional and moral. All four of these types of fitness are contributions you make to the wellness of all who know you.

6

FIRST AID

You may give birthday presents or Christmas presents, and that's great. Yet the greatest gift you can give someone is life, and first aid skills put that gift within your reach. First aid is not a substitute for professional medical care but it can keep a victim alive, as comfortable as possible, and minimize permanent damage.

First aid is needed most at life's most unpleasant moments. The victim may be upset and surrounded by upset people. It's easy for you to let your emotions run away with you too, but don't let that happen. You must stay calm and encourage others to stay calm, then act decisively.

Remember that courage is not the absence of fear, it is putting fear on hold while you act, and you can! To ensure that this happens, practice your first aid skills often. There are three stages you'll go through: when you can't get it right, when you can get it right, and when you can't get it wrong. Aim for the last stage and take a refresher from time to time to stay there.

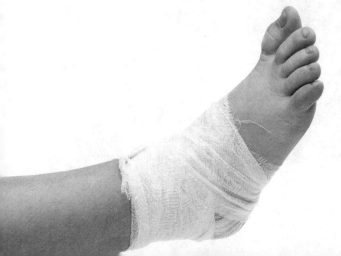

HANDS ONLY CPR

Hands-only CPR (Cardiopulmonary Resuscitation) is taught by the American Red Cross. It is a basic technique to get air into the victim's chest and use blood to carry that oxygen to the body's tissues.

I. If you see someone suddenly collapse, check the scene for safety. See if the victim responds to you by tapping them on the shoulder and shouting, "Are you OK?"

2. Briefly look at the chest for signs of breathing.

3. If they don't respond, call or send someone to call for help.

4. If the victim is not breathing or is gasping, prepare to give

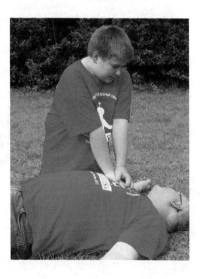

chest compressions. Kneel beside them and put the heel of one hand on the center of their chest. Place your other hand over that hand, lacing your fingers together. Position your shoulders directly over your hands keeping your arms straight and your fingers off the chest.

5. **Push hard and fast**, at least **2** inches and a rate of **I00** compressions per minute. Then let the chest rise completely before pressing down again. Don't take your hands off the chest, just your weight.

6. If victim is a child (I-8 years of age) technique remains the same, except you may only need one hand to give adequate chest compressions.

7. If victim is an infant (less than I year of age) everything is the same except chest compressions are done with 2 fingers in the middle of the chest just below the nipple line.

8. Keep going. Do not stop compressions until the victim shows an obvious sign of life (like breathing), the scene becomes unsafe, an Automatic External Defibrillator is ready, you are too exhausted to continue, or a

trained responder takes over.

9. If there are other bystanders around you can teach them to do compressions and take turns with you. Switch places about every 2 minutes to avoid fatigue.

Hands-only CPR is a great first step, but it is somewhat limited. Learning full CPR that involves rescue breathing and chest compressions will enable you to give greater levels of assistance in a wider variety of circumstances.

STOPPED BREATHING

The next level in CPR is to breathe for the victim. You need to use a protective barrier device or mask when performing Rescue Breaths. This skill should be taught by a qualified instructor and practiced on a simulator CPR dummy.

Clear the airway

1. After you have performed 30 chest compressions, open the victim's airway using the head-tilt, chin-lift maneuver.
   - Put your palm on the victim's forehead and gently tilt the head back.
   - With the other hand, gently lift

You need to use a protective barrier device or mask when performing Rescue Breaths.

the chin forward to open the airway.

2. Check quickly for normal breathing, taking no more than 5 to 10 seconds.
   - Look for chest rise.
   - Gasping is not considered to be normal breathing.

3. If the victim isn't breathing normally and you are trained in CPR, begin mouth-to-mouth Rescue Breathing.

Breathe for the victim

Rescue Breathing can be mouth-to-mouth breathing or mouth-to-nose breathing if the mouth is seriously injured or can't be opened.

1. With the airway open (using the head-tilt, chin-lift maneuver), **pinch the nostrils shut** for mouth-to-mouth breathing

and cover **the victim's mouth with yours**, making a seal.

2. Give the first of two rescue breaths, each over I second.
3. Deliver enough air to make the chest rise.
4. Watch to see if the chest rises.
5. If it does then give another breath.
    - If not, then repeat the head-tilt, chin-lift maneuver and try again.
    - If still no chest rise, consider Air Way Obstruction. *(See Choking)*
6. Resume chest compressions to restore circulation. *(See hands only CPR.)*
    - **Do not stop** chest compressions for more than I0 seconds at a time.
7. 30 chest compressions followed by 2 rescue breaths is considered I cycle.

8. If the victim has not begun moving after 5 cycles (about 2 minutes) and an AED is available, apply it and follow the prompts. *(See AED)*
9. Administer one shock then immediately resume Chest Compressions.
10. Continue for two more minutes before analyzing for a second shock.
    - The AED will prompt you.
    - Continue these cycles of **30:2** and then AED after each 5th cycle (about 2 minutes).
11. • Continue CPR until there are signs of movement or emergency medical personnel take over.
    - If there are other rescuers then take turns switching every 5 cycles (about 2 minutes).

Breathe for the young victim
Child (I-8 Yrs of age)
- Deliver enough air to make the chest rise, not too much.
- Same technique

Infant
- Deliver enough air to make the chest rise. Just what is in your cheeks.
- Cover infant's mouth and nose with your mouth.

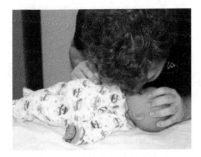

AED

AED or Automated External Defibrillation Device is used to reset the heart when it is in a **deadly rhythm**.

Just like you see on TV, the AED will shock the victim. The AED will decide whether to shock or not, depending upon if it would help the victim. The AED will guide you through the process, you only have to turn it on or open the lid.

- Call 9-1-1 or have someone else call 9-1-1. If two rescuers are present, one can provide CPR (cardiopulmonary resuscitation) while the other calls 9-1-1 and gets the AED.

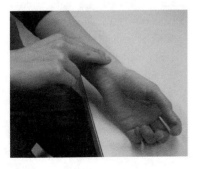

- Check the victim's breathing and pulse. If breathing and pulse are absent or irregular, prepare to use the AED as soon as possible.
- If no one knows how long the victim has been unconscious, or if an AED isn't readily available, do 2 minutes of CPR. Then use the AED (if you have one).
- After you use the AED, or if you don't have an AED, give CPR until emergency medical help arrives or until the victim begins to move. Try to limit pauses in CPR.
- After 2 minutes of CPR, you can use the AED again to check the victim's heart rhythm and give another shock, if needed. If a shock isn't needed then continue CPR.

Using an Automated External Defibrillator

AEDs are user-friendly devices that untrained bystanders can use to save the life of someone.

- **Before using an AED,** check for puddles or water near the victim who is unconscious. Move the victim to a dry area, and stay away from wetness when delivering shocks (water conducts electricity).
- **Turn on the AED's power.** The device will give you step-

by-step instructions. You'll hear voice prompts and may see prompts on a screen.

- **Expose the victim's chest.** If the victim's chest is wet, dry it. AEDs have sticky pads with sensors called electrodes. Apply the pads to the victim's chest as pictured on the AED's instructions.
- **Place one pad on the right center of the victim's chest above the nipple.**

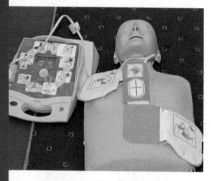

- **Place the other pad slightly below the other nipple and to the left of the ribcage.**
- *See photo here.*
- Make sure the sticky pads have good connection with the skin. If not, the machine may repeat the phrase, "check electrodes?"
- There are usually different pads for children than for adults – make sure you select the correct pads.
- If the victim has a lot of chest hair, you may have to trim it.

- If the victim is wearing a medication patch that's in the way, remove it and wipe the area clean.
- Remove metal necklaces and underwire bras. The metal may conduct electricity and cause burns.
- Check the victim for implanted medical devices, such as a pacemaker. Also check for body piercings.
- Move the defibrillator pads at least I inch away from implanted devices or piercings so the electric current can flow freely between the pads.
- Check that the wires from the electrodes are connected to the AED. Make sure no one is touching the victim, and then press the AED's "analyze" button. Stay clear while the machine checks the victim's heart rhythm.
- If a shock is needed, the AED will let you know when to deliver it. Stand clear of the victim and make sure others are clear before you push the AED's "shock" button.
- Start or resume CPR until emergency medical help arrives or until the victim begins to move. Stay with the victim until medical help arrives, and report all important information to them.

FIRST AID KITS

When you go on outings you should always have a personal first aid kit to treat minor problems. Unlike your Troop first aid kit, it is lightweight and small, just right for your pack. It is best to store yours in a re-sealable plastic bag. It should contain the following:

- 6 adhesive bandages
- 2 sterile, 3x3" gauze pads
- Small roll of adhesive tape
- 3x6" piece of moleskin
- Small bottle of alcohol-based hand sanitizing gel
- Small tube of triple antibiotic ointment
- Scissors
- Tweezers
- Disposable non-latex gloves
- PR breathing barrier
- Pencil and paper

Your Troop first-aid kit will contain a larger variety of supplies to handle more serious emergencies. It should be kept in plain view under the dining fly, clearly marked with a red cross on white.

Both personal and troop first aid kits should be checked at least once a year to make sure the supplies are present and that nothing has expired.

ACTION PLAN

There is no need to rush to treat a skin rash or a scraped knee. For more serious injuries, use the first aid action plan to make sure proper procedures are carried out in the best order.

Check the scene. You may spot clues to what caused the accident, and you may spot dangers that pose further hazard to the victim, bystanders or even you.

Call for help. Look for a bystander that has more experience, or someone that can call for medical assistance. In the backcountry send two or more people with as much of the following information as you can:

- Location of the victim
- Description of the illness or injuries
- Time the problem occurred
- Treatment the victim has received thus far
- Number of people with the victim and level of training

Approach safely. You're not being helpful if you become a victim, too! Introduce yourself to the victim and tell them you know first aid. Ask them if they need help. If they are

unconscious or too badly injured to respond, assume the answer is yes.

Provide urgent treatment. Begin by checking the victim's condition. Are they conscious and breathing? Is their heart beating? Is there severe bleeding? Do you see evidence of a cause such as allergies, a diabetic bracelet, a container of poison?

Triage: What do you do if you come upon more than one victim? Triage means to quickly evaluate the severity of condition of each victim, and prioritize which victim needs immediate treatment and how to ration your resources: rescuers, supplies, and transportation options.

Treat every victim for shock. When a victim is badly injured, their heart and lungs may not be providing enough blood and oxygen to body tissues. Shock requires rapid treatment. Its onset can be very sudden and people can go from alert talking and moving to acting strangely or slipping out of consciousness before you know it.

Decide where to go from here. If medical help will arrive shortly, keep the victim comfortable where they are and monitor their condition. *On a wilderness camping trip:* If in your best judgment the victim can travel and should hike to the nearest road, help them to travel. If the injuries are very serious, it is usually better to send two or more people to get medical help. At any rate, continue to monitor the victim closely and see if you need to take further action.

On the open water: Radio for help. GPS will be useful. Otherwise you need another plan to get help.

On a canoe trip: A Personal Locator Beacon or Satellite Phone is the best way to get help. Otherwise you need another plan to get help.

PROTECT YOURSELF

Always protect yourself from blood and bodily fluids:

- Wear gloves when you may be exposed to blood or bodily fluids, mucous membranes, or non-intact skin of an injured victim, or if someone is infected with a germ or bacteria that might infect you.
- Were eye protection when you may be exposed to splashing of blood or bodily fluids.
- Use a barrier device when giving mouth-to-mouth breaths – preferably a device with a one-way valve.

Proper way to remove gloves

- Grasp outside edge near wrist.
- Peel away from hand turning glove inside-out.
- Hold in opposite gloved hand.
- Slide ungloved finger under the wrist of the remaining glove, be careful not to touch the outside of the glove.
- Peel off from inside, creating a bag for both gloves
- Discard properly
- Wash hands thoroughly

Hand washing

- When decontaminating hands with an alcohol-based hand rub, apply product to hands and rub until hands are dry.
- When washing hands with soap and water, wet hands first with water, apply an amount of product recommended by the manufacturer to hands, and rub hands together vigorously for at least 15 seconds, covering all surfaces of the hands and fingers, including

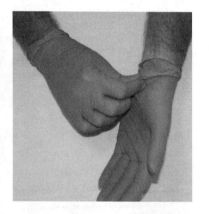
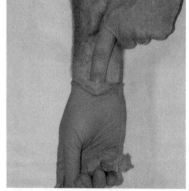
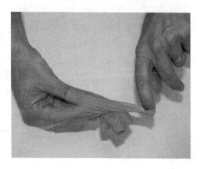

under the finger nails. Rinse hands with water and dry thoroughly with a disposable towel. Use towel to turn off the faucet
- Liquid, bar, leaflet or powdered forms of plain soap are acceptable when washing hands with a non-antimicrobial soap and water.

Treat every accident victim for shock even if there are no symptoms.

SHOCK

When a victim has been injured or subjected to another stress, the circulatory system may not be able to provide enough blood to all parts of the body. Shock is a life threatening condition.

Shock may have all, some, or none of these symptoms:
- Weakness
- Extreme thirst
- Restlessness or irritability
- Confusion, fear and dizziness
- Skin that is moist, cool, clammy and pale or gray
- A weak, quick pulse
- Blood pressure below normal
- Shallow and slow, rapid or deep or irregular breathing
- Nausea and vomiting

Treat every accident victim for shock even if there are no symptoms. Victims almost always experience some degree of shock though they might not be affected right away. Your quick response may prevent shock from setting in.

Treatment for shock includes sending for help, treating the immediate cause of the distress with first aid, helping the victim lie down and, if you don't suspect back, neck or head injuries or fractures of the leg or hip, raise the feet about a foot high to move blood from the legs to the vital organs. Keep the victim warm with blankets, sleeping bags or coats. Your remaining calm will increase the victim's ability to be calmer.

CHOKING

The usual cause of choking is foreign matter lodged in a victim's windpipe. A choking victim will probably panic leading to difficulty in getting their cooperation. Try to keep the victim calm so you can decide if your help is needed or if the victim can cough up the obstruction. "Are you choking?" That question is very effective. The victim may be coughing or gasping violently but if you get an answer, he is probably not choking. As long as he continues to cough, he is helping himself to clear any obstruction; a victim of choking usually cannot speak.

If all you get is a gesture or pointing to the throat or the universal sign of hands around the throat, or if the face is turning blue or the victim collapses, the victim probably cannot breathe. You need to perform the Heimlich maneuver at once! The Heimlich maneuver operates on the same principle as an air gun. You are using trapped air to pop out the airway obstruction.

- Start by first attempting five back blows by bending the person forward at the waist and giving 5 back blows between the shoulder blades
- If the back blows to do not result in the victim being able to breathe or cough then findthe proper stance - behind the victim with one of your feet planted firmly between the victim's feet and the other foot further back to brace yourself in case the victim loses consciousness.
- Wrap one of your arms around the victim and place your hand in a closed fist just slightly above his belly button.

- Place your other hand directly on top of the first.
- Squeeze the victim's abdomen in quick upward thrusts as many times as necessary to dislodge the object.
- If victim is a young child you may need to kneel behind them to perform Heimlich, otherwise no change in technique.

If you are unable to clear the victim's air passage, dial 9-1-1 immediately and continue to perform the Heimlich maneuver until help arrives. If victim loses consciousness then begin CPR, except each time before you give a breath look to see if you can see the object and pluck it out. NO BLIND FINGER SWEEPS!

Infant Choking

Do NOT perform these steps if the infant is coughing forcefully or has a strong cry. Strong coughs and cries can push the object out of the airway.

If your child is not coughing forcefully or does not have a strong cry, follow these steps:

- Lay the infant face down, along your forearm. Use your thigh or lap for support. Hold the infant's chest in your hand and jaw with your fingers. Point the infant's head downward, lower than the body.

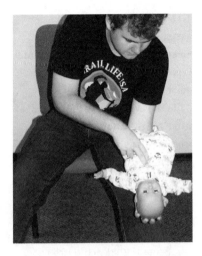

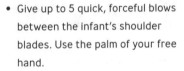

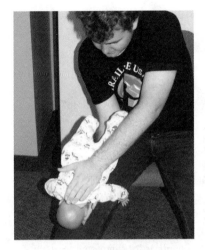

- Give up to 5 quick, forceful blows between the infant's shoulder blades. Use the palm of your free hand.

If the object does not come out of the airway after 5 blows:

- Turn the infant face up. Use your thigh or lap for support. Support the head.
- Place 2 fingers on the middle of his breastbone just below the nipples.
- Give up to 5 quick thrusts down, compressing the chest 1/3 to 1/2 the depth of the chest.
- Continue 5 back blows followed by 5 chest thrusts until the object is dislodged or the infant loses alertness (becomes unconscious).

If the child becomes unresponsive, stops breathing, or turns blue:

- Shout for help.

- Give infant CPR. Call 911 after 2 minutes of CPR.
- If you can see the object blocking the airway, try to remove it with your finger. **Try to remove an object only if you can see it. No blind finger sweeps!**

HEART ATTACK

Symptoms (may experience any or all of the following):

- Uncomfortable pressure, fullness or squeezing pain in the center of the chest.
- Prolonged pain in the upper abdomen.
- Discomfort or pain spreading beyond the chest to the shoulders, neck, jaw, teeth, or one or both arms.

- Shortness of breath.
- Lightheadedness, dizziness, fainting.
- Sweating.
- Nausea.

A heart attack generally causes chest pain for more than 15 minutes, but it can also have no symptoms at all. Many people who experience a heart attack have warning signs hours, days or weeks in advance.

Treatment:
- Call 911 - Don't wait more than 20 minutes for symptoms to resolve. **Time is Muscle!**
- Have victim chew and swallow an aspirin, unless they are allergic to aspirin.
- Give nitroglycerin, if prescribed.
- Begin CPR if the victim is unconscious.
- If you're with a victim who might be having a heart attack and they are unconscious, tell the 911 dispatcher and begin CPR.

STROKE

A stroke occurs when there's bleeding into the brain or when normal blood flow to the brain is blocked. Within minutes of being deprived of essential nutrients, brain cells start dying; a process that will continue over the next several hours.

Seek immediate medical assistance. A stroke is a true emergency. The sooner treatment is given; the more likely it is that damage can be minimized.

In the event of a possible stroke, use F.A.S.T. to help remember warning signs.
- **Face.** Does the face droop on one side trying to smile?
- **Arms.** Is one arm lower when trying to raise both arms?
- **Speech.** Can a simple sentence be repeated? Is speech slurred or strange?
- **Time.** During a stroke every minute counts. If you observe any of these signs, call 911 immediately.

SEIZURES

A seizure or convulsion is when a victim's body shakes rapidly and uncontrollably. During convulsions, the victim 's muscles contract and relax repeatedly. There are many different types of seizures. Some have mild symptoms and no body shaking.

Some seizures only cause a victim to have staring spells. These may go unnoticed. Specific symptoms depend on what part of the brain is involved. They occur suddenly and may include:
- Brief blackout followed by

period of confusion.

- Changes in behavior such as picking at one's clothing.
- Drooling or frothing at the mouth.
- Eye movements.
- Loss of bladder or bowel control.
- Mood changes such as sudden anger, unexplainable fear, panic, joy, or laughter.
- Shaking of the entire body.
- Sudden falling.
- Teeth clenching.
- Temporary halt in breathing.
- Uncontrollable muscle spasms with twitching and jerking limbs.

Symptoms may stop after a few seconds or minutes, or continue for 15 minutes. They rarely continue longer.

Causes

Seizures of all types are caused by disorganized and sudden electrical activity in the brain. Causes of seizures can include:

- Abnormal levels of sodium or glucose in the blood
- Brain infection, including meningitis
- Choking
- Drug abuse
- Electric shock
- Epilepsy
- Fever (particularly in young children)
- Head injury

- Heart disease
- Heat illness
- High fever
- Illegal Drugs
- Low blood sugar
- Poisoning
- Stroke
- Very high blood pressure
- Venomous bites and stings

Care

Most seizures stop by themselves. However, the patient can be hurt or injured during a seizure.

When a seizure occurs, the main goal is to protect the victim from injury.

- Lay the victim on the ground in a safe area. Clear the area of furniture or other sharp objects.
- Cushion the victim 's head.
- Loosen tight clothing, especially around the victim's neck.
- Turn the victim on their side. If vomiting occurs, this helps make sure that the vomit is not inhaled into the lungs.
- Look for a medical I.D. bracelet with seizure instructions.
- Stay with the victim until he or she recovers, or until help arrives
- If a baby or child has a seizure during a high fever, cool the child slowly with tepid water. Do not place the child in a cold bath.

- **Call 9II or your local emergency number if:**
- This is the first time the victim has had a seizure.
- A seizure lasts more than 2 to 5 minutes.
- The victim does not awaken or have normal behavior after a seizure.
- Another seizure starts soon after a seizure ends.
- The victim had a seizure in water.
- The victim is pregnant, injured, or has diabetes.
- The victim does not have a medical ID bracelet (instructions explaining what to do).
- There is anything different about this seizure compared to the victim 's usual seizures.

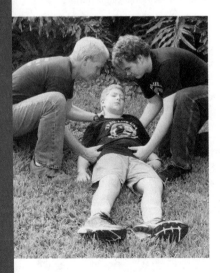

FAINTING

Fainting or Syncope is a temporary loss of consciousness. If you're about to faint, you'll feel dizzy, lightheaded, or nauseated. Your field of vision may "white out" or "black out." Your skin may be cold and clammy. You lose muscle control at the same time, and may fall down.

Fainting usually happens when your blood pressure drops suddenly, causing a decrease in blood flow to your brain. It is more common in older people. Some causes of fainting include

- Heat or dehydration
- Emotional distress
- Standing up too quickly
- Certain medicines
- Drop in blood sugar
- Heart problems

When someone faints, make sure that the airway is clear and check for breathing. The victim should stay lying down for I0-I5 minutes. Most people recover completely. Fainting is usually nothing to worry about, but it can sometimes be a sign of a serious problem. If you faint, it's important to see your health care provider and find out why it happened.

LOW BLOOD SUGAR

Low Blood Sugar or Hypoglycemia is a condition that occurs when your blood sugar (glucose) is too low. Blood sugar below 70 mg/dL is considered low.

Causes

Low blood sugar is most commonly seen in people with diabetes who are taking insulin or other medicines to control their diabetes. Hypoglycemia in people who do not have diabetes may be caused by: Drinking alcohol or skipping a meal.

Symptoms

Symptoms you may have when your blood sugar gets too low include:

- Double vision or blurry vision
- Fast or pounding heartbeat
- Feeling cranky or acting aggressively
- Feeling nervous
- Headache
- Hunger
- Shaking or trembling
- Sweating
- Tingling or numbness of the skin
- Tiredness or weakness
- Trouble sleeping
- Unclear thinking

Sometimes your blood sugar may be too low, even if you do not have symptoms. If your blood sugar gets too low, you may:

- Faint
- Have a seizure
- Go into a coma (Insulin shock)

Treatment

Treatment depends on the cause. Eat something that has about 15 grams of carbohydrates. Examples are:

- 3 glucose tablets
- A 1/2 cup (4 ounces) fruit juice or regular, non-diet soda
- 5 or 6 hard candies
- 1 tablespoon sugar, plain or dissolved in water
- 1 tablespoon honey or syrup

Wait about 15 minutes before eating any more. Be careful not to eat too much. This can cause high blood sugar.

Follow with a good meal or at least a good source of protein.

ALLERGIC REACTION (ANAPHYLACTIC SHOCK)

Anaphylaxis is a severe, whole-body allergic reaction to a chemical that has become an allergen, and can be life-threatening. Anaphylaxis can occur in response to any allergen.

Common causes include:

- Drug allergies
- Insect bites/stings
- Food allergies; eggs, fish, shellfish, soy, tree nuts, peanuts, and wheat are the most common.

Symptoms

Symptoms can come on quickly:

- Abnormal (high-pitched) breathing sounds
- Chest discomfort or tightness
- Cough
- Difficulty breathing
- Difficulty swallowing
- Hives, itchiness
- Nausea or vomiting
- Rapid weak pulse
- Swelling of the face, eyes, or tongue
- Unconsciousness

Treatment

- Call 9ll immediately.
- Check the victim's airway, breathing, and circulation
- Be calm and reassure the victim.
- If the victim has emergency allergy medicine, help the victim take or inject the medication. Antihistamine or Epinephrine injection.
- Avoid oral medication if the victim is having difficulty breathing.
- Take steps to prevent shock.

Possible Complications

- Airway blockage
- Cardiac arrest
- Respiratory arrest
- Shock

Epinephrine injection

CUTS AND SCRAPES

The skin is your primary defense against germs. When it gets broken, bacteria penetrate that outer wall and can cause infection.

Begin treating minor cuts and scrapes by thoroughly cleaning the wound with mild anti-bacterial soap and water. You can use sterilized tweezers to remove any debris that remains embedded in the wound after rinsing to reduce the risk of an infection. If all the debris can't be removed, a trip to the emergency room will be necessary.

Cleaning the wound may induce bleeding. If so, use gauze or a clean cloth to apply gentle, continuous pressure for 5 – 10 minutes until the bleeding stops.

Apply a triple antibiotic ointment such as Neosporin™ to keep the wound from getting infected and speed healing. Dress the wound with a bandage or sterile gauze to keep out dirt and bacteria. Clean the wound and change the dressing daily. If the wound is very deep or the bleeding is profuse, it may require stitches in order to heal properly. This should only be done by a health care professional.

SPLINTERS

1. **Clean Wound** - Clean the area with mild soap and water.
   - If a small splinter doesn't hurt, let the splinter work its way out over a few days.
   - If it does hurt, touch the area gently with sticky tape and pull away carefully.
2. **Remove Larger Splinter**
   - Clean a small needle and tweezers with alcohol.
   - If you can see the end of the splinter, grip it with the tweezers and gently pull out the entire splinter.
   - If none of the splinter is sticking out, follow the path of the splinter with the needle. Open the skin and expose enough of the splinter to remove it with tweezers.
   - Clean wound area again. Apply a bandage and antibiotic ointment.

Most splinters do not need the care of a health care provider, but it is important to prevent possible infection *(see puncture wounds, below)*.

BITE WOUNDS

A bite from a wild animal such as a raccoon or squirrel may require an immediate shot to prevent the possibility of rabies, seek medical advice. Domestic animals can carry rabies as well, if the animal is unknown to victim, find owner and get shot records. If you can't find an owner, seek medical advice.

Usually, a bite from a domestic pet may be painful but rarely requires a visit to the emergency room. Unless obvious bodily harm was sustained, simple precautionary treatment is enough. Use the same procedures for a Human bite.

- Use anti-bacterial soap and water to thoroughly clean the bite wound.
- Apply antibiotic ointment such as Neosporin™ to prevent infection.
- If the injury resulted in broken skin, dress it with a sterile bandage and replace the dressing frequently.
- If the bite is deep, the victim may need to be treated for a puncture wound.

PUNCTURE WOUNDS

A puncture wound does not usually bleed profusely. While painful it may appear harmless because the skin around the puncture may close. Yet puncture wounds are very susceptible to infection and if untreated can result in serious complications.

Punctures of the foot caused by stepping on a nail through a shoe are extremely prone to infection. If the puncture is caused by stepping on a nail or glass that has been exposed to the elements, it would be wise to see a doctor who may recommend a tetanus shot or booster.

Animal bites resulting in a puncture wound are serious. If the bleeding is heavy or the wound or what produced it appears unsanitary, clean the injured area thoroughly with mild anti-bacterial soap and water and seek medical assistance as soon as possible.

If the injury is minor, clean it with soap and water and apply an antibiotic ointment such as Neosporin™ to prevent infection. Dress the wound with sterile bandage and replace the dressing frequently. Keep watch for the next few days, and if you notice persistent redness or puffiness or if the wound starts to ooze, have the victim consult a doctor right away.

(Neosporin™ is a registered trademark)

MOUTH AND TOOTH INJURIES

If your tooth is broken, chipped, or fractured, see your dentist as soon as possible. Otherwise your tooth could be damaged further or become infected, possibly causing you to end up losing the tooth.

In the meantime, try the following self-care measures:

- If the tooth is painful, take acetaminophen or another pain reliever. Rinse your mouth with salt water.
- If the break has caused a sharp or jagged edge, cover it with a piece of wax, paraffin, or chewing gum.
- If you must eat, eat soft foods and avoid biting down on the broken tooth.

Knocked out tooth

If a permanent tooth is knocked out, get emergency dental care. It's sometimes possible to successfully re-implant permanent teeth that have been knocked out, but only if you follow the steps below immediately — before you see a dentist.

- Handle your tooth by the top or crown only, not the roots.
- Don't rub the tooth or scrape it to remove debris. This damages the root surface.
- Gently rinse your tooth in a bowl of tap water. Don't hold it under running water.
- Try to replace your tooth in the socket. If it doesn't go all the way into place, bite down slowly and gently on gauze or a moistened tea bag to help keep it in place. Hold the tooth in place until you see your dentist.
- If you can't replace your tooth in the socket, immediately place it in some milk, your own saliva or a warm, mild saltwater solution — 1/4 teaspoon salt to 1 quart water.

Bleeding of the Mouth

- Wash your hands well with soap and water, if available.
- Put on medical gloves, if available, before applying pressure to the wound. If gloves are not available, use many layers of fabric, plastic bags, or whatever you have between your hands and the wound.

- Have the victim hold their own hand over the wound, if possible, and apply pressure to the injured area.
- Use your bare hands to apply pressure only as a last resort.

Have the victim sit up and tilt their head forward with the chin down. This will help any blood drain out of the mouth, not down the back of the throat. Swallowing blood can cause vomiting.

- **Remove any visible objects** that are easy to remove. Remove chewing gum if it is present.
- **Remove any jewelry** from the general area of the wound.
- **Press firmly** on the wound with a clean cloth or the cleanest material available. If there is an object in the wound, apply pressure around the object, not directly over it.
- **Apply steady pressure for a full 15 minutes. Use a clock to time the 15 minutes.** It can seem like a long time. Resist the urge to peek after a few minutes to see whether bleeding has stopped. If blood soaks through the cloth, apply another one without lifting the first.
- **Inner lip bleeding.** Press the bleeding site against the teeth or jaw or place a rolled or folded piece of gauze or clean cloth between the lip and gum.
- **Tongue bleeding.** Squeeze or press the bleeding site with gauze or a piece of clean cloth.
- **Inner cheek bleeding.** Place rolled gauze or a piece of clean cloth between the wound and the teeth.
- Avoid spitting, using any form of tobacco, and using straws, which can make bleeding worse.

SEVERE BLEEDING

A severe cut can kill in a matter of minutes. Immediately ask someone to summon help, but if it is just you and the victim, do not leave them before beginning first aid.

With a clean cloth or sterile dressing, use the palm of your hand to apply firm continuous pressure directly over the wound for 20 minutes. A tourniquet may be used if unable to stop bleeding but, as a last resort only. Use an elastic bandage if you have one to secure the pad tightly over the source of the bleeding.

If you don't have a clean cloth, use whatever is available. They will bleed to death long before they would ever become infected!

After the bleeding stops, hold the pad in place with a sterile bandage.

Bind the pad firmly but not tightly enough to cut off circulation. Immobilize and elevate the extremity above the heart.

When the bandage is on a limb, check farther down the limb every few minutes for a pulse, for warmth, feeling and color. If you can't feel a pulse or if fingers or toes are numb, pale or cold, the bandage needs to be loosened.

If a pad becomes soaked with blood, put a fresh pad over it and continue applying pressure. Do not remove a blood soaked pad.

As with all other injuries requiring first aid, treat the victim for shock.

INTERNAL BLEEDING OR ABDOMINAL PAIN

Call 9ll if:

- You have pain and tenderness to the touch in the lower right abdomen with fever and/or vomiting. These may be signs of appendicitis. Seek medical attention!
- You are pregnant and have abdominal pain or vaginal bleeding. This may be a sign of an ectopic pregnancy or miscarriage. Seek medical attention!

Treat Symptoms

- For heartburn from gastro-esophageal reflux disease (GERD), take an over-the-counter antacid.
- For constipation, take a mild stool softener or laxative.
- For pain, take acetaminophen. Avoid aspirin and ibuprofen because they can cause stomach irritation or bleeding.

Call a Doctor if the victim has:

- Severe abdominal pain or pain that lasts several days
- Nausea, vomiting, fever, or inability to keep food down for several days
- Bloody stools, or black tarry stools
- Vomits blood
- Difficulty breathing
- Blow or injury to the abdomen in the days before the pain started

OBJECTS IN THE EYE

The best way to get objects out of your eye is not to get them in the first place. That's why there are safety glasses or goggles you wear while using certain types of tools and machines that throw out debris.

If someone does get something in their eye, encourage them not to rub it. If the victim wears contact lenses, they should be removed. Ask the victim to blink the eyes rapidly. This may permit tears to wash the eye out. Flushing the eyes with eye wash, or if not available, clean water from a tap, water bottle or cup are also useful. If the object will not wash out, cover the affected eye with a dry, sterile gauze pad and get the victim to a doctor.

Certain liquid chemicals in the eye can cause discomfort or damage and should be treated by flushing the eye under a tap. The length of time recommended is often stated on the chemical container.

BLISTERS

The best way to deal with blisters is to prevent them in the first place. While you are hiking, wear shoes or boots that fit you well and have been properly broken in. If your socks get sweaty or wet, change them. Wear work gloves while working outdoors to protect your hands. If you get a blister while hiking, cut a piece of moleskin slightly larger than the blister patch. The moleskin will help protect the spot.

Do not pop blisters unless you have to. Breaking the skin increases the risk of infection. If you must pop them, sterilize a needle with a flame and stick the blister close to its base to drain the fluid. Apply antibiotic ointment and protect with a dressing.

BURNS

A burn victim will require different type of care depending on the type and extent of his injury. Burns vary greatly from sunburn to life-threatening 3rd degree burns caused by open flames, chemicals or electric shock. Treat the burn according to its type.

First Degree Burns

Symptoms: First degree burns are usually caused by over exposure to the sun (sunburn) and accompanied by redness and some swelling of the skin. The best way to treat sunburn is avoid it by apply sunscreen with an SPF of 30 or greater every 2 hours or more if sweating or swimming. Wearing a wide brim hat, sunglasses, long sleeves and long pants can help as well.

Treatment: Treat a minor burn by first cooling the affected area. If possible, keep the injury under cool running water for at least 10 minutes.

If running water is not available place the burned area in a container of cold water such as a bucket, tub or even a deep dish. Using a cool, wet compress made of clean cloth will also work if nothing else is available.

Keeping the burn cool will reduce pain and minimize the swelling. If the injury is on the part of a body where jewelry or snug clothing is present, carefully remove them before it begins to swell. Apply a moisturizing lotion or Aloe Vera extract and dress the burnt area with loosely wrapped sterile gauze.

Second Degree Burns

Symptoms: Second degree burns will result in deeper, more intense redness of the skin as well as swelling and blistering.

Treatment: This type of burn should be treated just as a first degree burn but because the damage to the skin is more extensive, extra care should be taken to avoid infection and excessive scarring. Replace the dressing daily and keep the wound clean. If a blister breaks use mild soap and warm water to rinse the area. Apply antibiotic cream such as Neosporin™ to prevent infection before redressing in sterile gauze.

(Neosporin™ is a registered trademark)

Third Degree Burns

Symptoms: Third degree burns may appear and feel deceptively harmless as the victim may not feel much pain due to complete destruction of all layers of skin and tissue as well as nerve endings. The damaged area may appear charred or ash-color and will instantly start to blister or "peel".

Treatment: If the victim's clothing is on fire, tell them: Stop, Drop, and Roll. If they panic and run: douse them with a non-flammable liquid. Dial 9-1-1. Do not remove burnt clothing from the victim as this will expose open wounds to the elements and potential infection. If possible, cover the victim's injuries with wet sterile cloth to reduce the pain and swelling. Do not apply any antibiotic cream or other lotions. If you notice that the victim is going into shock and loses consciousness, you will need to perform CPR and treat for shock.

FRACTURES

A broken bone is not always obvious. It is important not to mistake a broken bone for a bruise or sprain. Typical symptoms of a fracture are:

- Immediate and excessive swelling
- Injured area appears deformed
- The bone has pierced the skin or bleeding is present (known as a "compound fracture")

- The farthest point of the injured limb turns blue or is numb to the touch
- Even slight movement or contact to the injured area causes excessive pain.

Immobilize the broken bone with a splint. A functional splint can be made of almost any material (sticks, plastic, etc.) as long as it is rigid and is longer than the broken bone. To apply the splint simply lay it along the broken bone and wrap it against the limb with gauze or a length of cloth, starting at a point farthest from the body. Do not wrap it too tight as this may cut off blood flow.

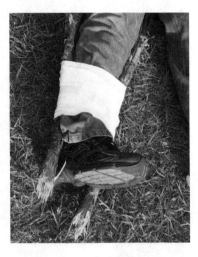

If the break is in the upper or lower arm, loosely wrap a magazine or a thick newspaper around the break and use a sling fashioned

from gauze or a strip of cloth to keep the elbow immobilized.

A break in the lower or upper part of the leg requires two splints, one on each side of the leg (or at least the shin). If suitable material is not available, you can use the victim's healthy leg as a makeshift splint.

In the case of a compound fracture, do not attempt to push the exposed bone back. Splint around it to not further aggravate any internal bleeding.

As much as possible, keep the victim from moving and until an ambulance arrives, remember ICE:

"I" is for **ice** - if possible apply an ice pack or ice cubes to the injured area. This will keep down the swelling, reduce pain and, can help to slow bleeding. Apply ice for 20 minutes at a time and repeat every 3-6 hours.

"C" is for **compression** - if the wound is bleeding, apply direct pressure with a clean cloth to reduce blood flow. (Except in situations where direct pressure would be on a compound fracture that could increase internal damage.)

"E" is for **elevation** - try to keep the injured area as high above heart level as possible. This will reduce blood flow to the injury and minimize swelling.

A broken collarbone or clavicle is a common injury; it connects the upper part of your breastbone (sternum) to your shoulder blade (scapula). Common causes of a broken collarbone include falls onto a shoulder, sports injuries and trauma from traffic accidents.

- **Ice** - Applying ice to the affected area during the first two to three days following a collarbone break can help control pain and swelling.
- **Immobilization** -Restricting the movement of any broken bone is critical to healing. To immobilize a broken collarbone, you'll likely need to wear an arm sling. In some cases a figure-eight strap that fits around both your shoulders to help keep the bone in place.
- **Medications** -To reduce pain and inflammation, use over-the-counter pain relievers.
- **Get to doctor for treatment.**

Broken Ankle

- **Ice** - Applying ice to the affected area during the first two to three days following a break can help control pain and swelling.
- **Immobilization** -Restricting the movement of any broken bone is critical to healing. To immobilize

a broken ankle, you will likely need to wrap it in a figure-eight. to help keep the bone in place.
- **Medications** -To reduce pain and inflammation, use over-the-counter pain relievers.
- **Get to doctor for treatment.**

SPRAINS

Your ligaments are tough, elastic-like bands that connect bone to bone and hold your joints in place. A sprain is an injury to a ligament caused by tearing of the fibers of the ligament. It can have a partial tear, or it can be completely torn apart.

Of all the sprains, ankle and knee sprains occur most often. Sprained ligaments swell rapidly and are painful. Generally, the greater the pain and swelling, the more severe the injury is. For most minor sprains, you probably can treat the injury yourself. Follow the instructions for R.I.C.E.:

- **Rest** the injured limb. Your doctor may recommend not putting any weight on the injured area for 48 hours. But don't avoid all activity. Even with an ankle sprain, you can usually still exercise other muscles to minimize deconditioning.
- **Ice** the area. Use a cold pack, a slush bath of ice water or a

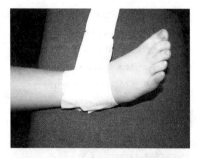

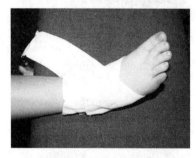

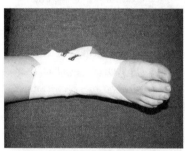

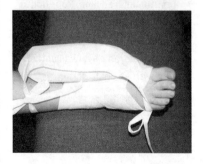

compression sleeve filled with cold water to help limit swelling after an injury. Try to ice the area as soon as possible after the injury and continue to ice it for 15 to 20 minutes, four to eight times a day, for the first 48 hours or until swelling improves. If you use ice, be careful not to use it too long, as this could cause tissue damage.

- **Compress** the area with an elastic wrap or bandage. Compressive wraps or sleeves made from elastic or neoprene are best.
- **Elevate** the injured limb above your heart whenever possible to help prevent or limit swelling.

After two days, gently begin using the injured area. You should feel a gradual, progressive improvement. Over-the-counter pain relievers, such as ibuprofen (Advil™, Motrin™, others) and acetaminophen (Tylenol™, others), may be helpful to manage pain during the healing process.

(Advil™, Motrin™ and Tylenol ™ are registered trademarks)

See your doctor if your sprain isn't improving after two or three days.

Get emergency medical assistance if:

- You're unable to bear weight on the injured leg, the joint feels unstable or numb, or you can't use the joint. This may mean the ligament was completely torn. On the way to the doctor, apply a cold pack.

- You develop redness or red streaks that spread out from the injured area. This means you may have an infection.
- You have re-injured an area that has been injured a number of times in the past.
- You have a severe sprain. Inadequate or delayed treatment may contribute to long-term joint instability or chronic pain.

TRANSPORTING METHODS

There are many ways to carry an injured victim. Choose one that is considerate of the severity and type of injury. Determine your resources: number and size of rescuers, materials available, also size of victim, distance that you have to move them and the geography and topography. **Make sure you don't get hurt or drop the victim; be careful.**

Walking assists:

Conscious - one rescuer
- Place their arm around your shoulders and hold that hand.
- Place your free hand around the victim's waist.
- Let the victim set the pace and be prepared to stop frequently.

Unconscious - two rescuer
- Both rescuers grasp the belt or waistband of the unconscious victim.
- Pull to lift the victim's upper body.

Pack strap carry

One rescuer

Two rescuers

- With both rescuers facing each other, squat next to the victim and place their arm around your shoulders and hold that hand.
- Slowly stand to lift victim, keep your back straight and use your legs to help avoid injury
- Move forward dragging the victim's legs

Dragging assists: One rescuer

Blanket - Conscious or Unconscious

- Lay a blanket, coat or tarp on the ground close to the victim.
- Roll or lift the victim carefully onto the blanket.
- Keep the head and neck aligned while moving the victim.
- Keep enough material to pull with,

your grasp of the material should be about 2 feet from the victim's head
- Keep your back as straight as possible while moving the victim.

Shoulder - Conscious or Unconscious

- Grasp the victim's clothing underneath their shoulders.
- Support the victim's head by keeping an arm along the side of it.
- Pull the victim keeping the body aligned.

Ankle - Conscious or Unconscious

- Grasp the victim by the ankles or pant cuffs.
- Keep your back as straight as possible.
- Drag the victim in a straight line.
- This carry is not preferred, as it

Blanket rescue

Shoulder rescue

Ankle rescue

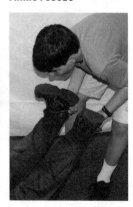

does not support the head or neck and should only be performed slowly and on smooth ground or grass.

Two Rescuer Carries:

Two-hand seat - Conscious or Unconscious

- While facing each other squat on each side of the victim keeping your backs as straight as possible.
- Reach under the victim's shoulders with one arm and under the knees with the other.
- Grab onto your partner's wrists, arm, or shoulder and hold tightly.
- If victim is conscious they can place their arms around rescuers necks
- Lift victim slowly using your legs, keep back straight.

Four-hand seat - Conscious

- Face your partner and hold your right wrist with your left hand. Grab your partner's left wrist with your right hand. You should have a seat for the victim to sit.
- Lower yourselves by bending your knees, keeping your wrists interlocked so the victim can sit.
- If victim is conscious they can place their arms around rescuers necks
- Lift victim slowly using your legs, keep back straight.

Two-hand seat

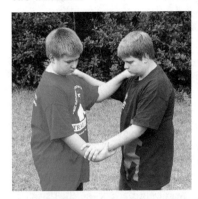

Four-hand seat

Chair carry - Conscious or Unconscious

- Help or place the victim onto a sturdy chair.
- The conscious victim should fold their arms across the chest to prevent injury.
- Tie an unconscious victim to the back of the chair using a rope, blanket or piece of clothing.
- Stand at the sides of the chair. Grab the back of the chair's sides with your palms facing the victim's back.
- Tilt the chair onto its rear legs.
- Each rescuer should grab the front leg with remaining hand.
- Lift the chair off the ground and start walking. **Do not walk backwards.**

Chair carry

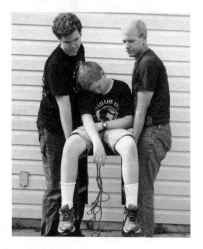

Human Stretcher carry for 3-6 Rescuers

- 3 - 6 Trailmen stand on both sides of the victim
- Squat or kneel on one knee facing each other
- Link hands/wrists under victim
- Lift victim slowly using your legs; keep back straight.

Improvised Stretcher: Blanket and Shirt/Coat

- Locate 2 poles that can hold the victim's weight, tent poles, car rack poles or two sturdy pieces of wood.
- Then locate a blanket, unzipped sleeping bag, tarp, shirts, pants, or coats; that are able to hold the victim's weight.
- Using clothing, zip or button it and stick the poles through the bottom and through though sleeves or pant legs. You need enough garments to cover the height of victim.

- Spread the blanket out on the ground. Place I "pole" about I foot from the center of the blanket.

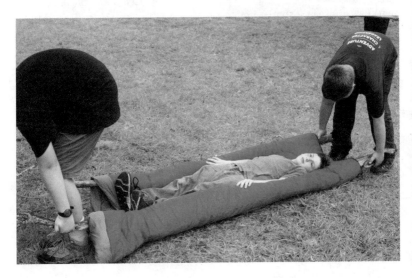

- Fold the shorter end of the blanket over the first pole.
- Put the second pole about 2 feet from the first pole. Or adjust size to accommodate victim and blanket.
- Fold both halves of the blanket over the second pole.
- Trailmen should stand at each end of stretcher
- Squat down and grasp the poles. Trailman at the head should face away from victim.
- Lift victim slowly using your legs, keep back straight

HEAD INJURY

The majority of minor head injuries caused by a small fall or a bumping of the head which may cause a bump or a bruise or a short-term headache are not dangerous. It is very important to pay close attention to head injuries, especially those with the following symptoms:

- Excessive bleeding from an open wound, ears or nose.
- Clear fluid coming from ears or nose.
- Loss of consciousness
- Prolonged disorientation, apparent memory loss, irritability, slurred speech, dizziness, or drowsiness

- Unequal pupil size, blurred or double vision
- Nausea or vomiting
- Weakness in hands or feet
- Interruption of breathing or change in rhythm

If you detect any of these symptoms, you should assume the victim has sustained serious head trauma and needs medical attention. Dial 9-1-1 immediately, and until the ambulance arrives:

- If possible, place the victim in a dim, quiet area.
- Lay the victim down, head and shoulders slightly elevated.
- If the wound is bleeding, dress it with gauze or clean cloth.
- Apply ice for 20 minutes every 2-4 hours
- Do not leave the victim unattended during the first 24 hours
- Awaken and check for alertness every 2 hours
- If the victim loses consciousness, you may need to perform CPR.

NECK AND SPINAL INJURIES

If you suspect a back or neck (spinal) injury, do not move the victim. Permanent paralysis and other serious complications can result. Assume the victim has a spinal injury if:

- There's evidence of a head injury and any change in the level of consciousness
- The victim complains of severe pain in their neck or back
- They won't move their neck
- An injury has exerted substantial force on the back or head – especially a fall from elevation
- The victim either exhibits or complains of weakness, numbness or paralysis or lacks control of limbs, bladder or bowels
- The neck or back is twisted or positioned oddly

If you suspect someone has a spinal injury:

- Call 9II or emergency medical help.
- Keep the victim still. Place heavy towels on both sides of the neck or hold the head and neck.
- Provide as much first aid as possible without moving the victim's head, neck or back.
- If the victim is unconscious and shows no signs of circulation (breathing, coughing or movement), begin chest compression, but do not tilt the head back to open the airway. Use your fingers to gently grasp the jaw and lift it forward.
- If the victim is wearing a helmet, don't remove it.
- If you absolutely must roll the victim because he or she is vomiting, choking on blood or in danger of further injury, you need at least one other Trailman. Work together to keep the victim's head, neck and back aligned while rolling the victim onto one side. Roll them like a log.

NOSEBLEED

A human nose is rich with small fragile blood vessels which are susceptible to damage. A nosebleed may be caused by a fall, a strike to the nose, or even from breathing excessively dry air.

If the nosebleed is not a symptom of a more serious injury, it is rarely dangerous and can usually be stopped by continuous pressure.

- Do NOT tilt the victim's head backward.
- Have the victim sit or stand upright to slow down the flow of blood.
- Loosen any tight clothing around the victim's neck.
- If possible, have the victim spit out excess saliva - swallowing may disturb the clot and cause nausea.
- Pinch the nostrils shut and press the tip of the nose against the bones of the face.
- Maintain pressure for 5 to I0 minutes.

- Once the bleeding has stopped, the victim should avoid blowing his nose or otherwise straining himself for at least an hour.

If the victim's nose continues to bleed or if the blood flow appears to be excessive, or if the victim feels weak or faint, the damage may be more serious than it appears. You should call 9-1-1 or take him to the nearest emergency room as soon as possible.

POISONOUS PLANTS

Poison ivy, poison oak, poison sumac, and stinging nettle are the most common skin irritant plants found in North America.

Poison ivy, poison oak, and poison sumac have oily sap in their leaves, stems and roots which may irritate your skin. If you can wash the sap off with soap and water within ten minutes, you can spare yourself a lot of misery. Remember that the oil clings to clothing too, so make sure any clothing that comes into contact with these plants gets a thorough washing.

Stinging nettles inject a combination of chemicals (mostly histamine) that cause a stinging sensation and rash. Due to the complex mixture of irritants, treating the discomfort is more complicated. Common anti-itch drugs may or may not help. As a backup, calamine lotion often brings relief.

For any of these plants, avoid scratching the skin! If the reaction is severe, if the eyes or genital region is affected, or if parts of the plant were chewed or swallowed,

Poison Ivy

Poison Oak

seek immediate medical attention.

Prevention: Wearing long sleeves and long pants can help protect from the plant oils.

Some people are especially allergic to poison ivy, poison oak or poison sumac. For them, smoke from burning these plants or even a strong wind passing over them may cause a reaction. Dead plants and dried roots can still cause irritation.

Poison ivy can vary somewhat in its appearance. It may be very shiny or not. The plant may have white berries. It is best to have a Trail Guide point out several examples of poison ivy on hikes or campouts so that you develop a feel for the plant.

Generally poison oak is more toxic than poison ivy, and poison sumac is so toxic as to be extremely dangerous.

SPIDER BITES

Most spider bites cause relatively minor pain and itching that soon go away. Some spider bites are more serious.

A bite from a brown recluse spider may not hurt at once, but may cause pain, redness, and swelling at the wound within two to eight hours. An open sore is likely to form and the victim may suffer fever, chills, nausea, joint pain, vomiting and a faint rash.

The bite of a female black widow spider might cause sharp pain and redness at the wound. Symptoms may include sweating, nausea, vomiting, stomach pain, and cramps, severe muscle pain and spasms, and shock. It may cause difficulty breathing.

Treat all spider bite victims for shock, recheck the bite area periodically, and have them seen by a doctor as soon as possible.

SCORPION STINGS

Scorpion stings although painful are mostly harmless. As many as 1,500 species of scorpions have been described worldwide, but only about 30 of these are considered dangerous. In the United States, only the bark scorpion, native to Arizona, New Mexico and the California side of the Colorado River, has venom potent enough to cause severe symptoms. Elsewhere, lethal scorpion stings occur predominantly in Mexico, South America, parts of Africa, the Middle East and India.

Scorpion stings are most serious in young children, older adults and pets. In the United States, healthy adults usually don't need treatment for scorpion stings, but if a child is stung, always get immediate medical care.

Symptoms

Children who have been stung by a bark scorpion might experience:

- Pain, which can be intense, numbness and tingling in the area around the sting, but little or no swelling
- Muscle twitching or thrashing
- Unusual head, neck and eye movements
- Drooling
- Sweating
- Restlessness or excitability and sometimes inconsolable crying

Adults are more likely to experience:

- Rapid breathing
- High blood pressure
- Increased heart rate
- Muscle twitching
- Weakness

When to see a doctor

It's always best to be safe. Anyone stung should follow these guidelines:

- Make a note of the time stung and, if known, a description of the scorpion.
- Get immediate medical care for any child stung by a scorpion.
- If you've been stung, get prompt care if you begin to experience widespread symptoms.
- If you're concerned about a scorpion sting — even if your reaction is minor — call your local poison control center for advice.
- Seek medical attention right away if stung while traveling in another country.

SNAKE BITE

If someone is bitten by a snake or lizard that is known or thought to be possibly venomous, call 9II or other emergency services immediately. Do not wait for symptoms to develop. Symptoms may progress from mild to severe rapidly.

If you are not sure what type of snake or lizard bit you, take a picture of it. But do not do this if it will delay treatment or put someone at risk for additional bites.

- Remain calm and try to rest quietly.
- If you are not sure what type of snake or lizard bit you, **call the Poison Control Center 800-222-1222** to help identify the snake or lizard and find out what to do next.
- Remove any jewelry. The limbs might swell, making it more difficult to remove the jewelry

after swelling begins.

- Use a pen to mark the edge of the swelling around the bite every 15 minutes. This will help your doctor estimate how the venom is moving in your body.

TICKS

Ticks are small, hard-shelled creatures related to spiders that bury their heads in the skin. Some are larger and easier to spot, others are tiny "seed ticks" that are hard to spot during a casual inspection.

The best way to treat ticks is to properly apply repellant in the first place. Wearing long sleeves and long pants can help too. Sometimes we forget and or miss a spot and ticks are always ready to remind us!

Remove ticks with tweezers, grasping the tick close to the skin and gently pulling until the tick comes out. If you squeeze, twist or jerk the tick it may cause the tick's mouthparts to break off in the wound and result in an infection or blood poisoning.

Wash the wound with soap and water and apply a good triple antibiotic ointment.

Ticks may spread Lyme disease, Rocky Mountain spotted fever or other illnesses. If you have flulike symptoms, develop a rash or otherwise feel unwell in the following days or weeks, see your doctor.

CHIGGERS

Chiggers, if you even see them, look like tiny red dots. Feeling them is much easier! Using repellant sprays correctly is far less trouble than resisting the urge to scratch the small bumps that form on the skin. Wearing long sleeves and long pants can help, too. If chiggers get to you, cover the bites with calamine lotion or dab them with clear fingernail polish.

INSECT STINGS

If you are stung by a bee or hornet, the stinger and poison sack are often left in the wound. Remove the stinger by scraping it out with a drivers' license, credit card or the side of a knife blade. If you try to pinch it out or scrape it with a finger, you may push more venom into the wound. An ice pack may help reduce pain and swelling.

Anyone that has trouble breathing after an insect sting must be treated immediately for anaphylactic shock. Call 911 or your local emergency number. If the victim has a kit for treating anaphylactic shock such as an EpiPen, follow the instructions in assisting them to use it.

FIRE ANTS

Fire ants are not native to North America, but unfortunately they are spreading in the southeastern and southwestern US.

The best way to treat fire ant stings is not to get any! Keep your shoes on when playing near fire ant mounds. If you come across one, don't poke at it or play with it. You will easily recognize their mounds because they can grow up to 18 inches high and over 2 feet wide.

Fire ant stings cause sharp pain and burning. If the victim steps on a fire ant mound they may be stung several times at once. Each sting will turn into an itchy white blister over the next day.

Tell an adult immediately. The venom in the fire ant stings may cause quite a bit of swelling and a doctor may need to look at it to make sure the victim is not having an allergic reaction.

If the victim develops hives (red patches on the skin that itch and sting), nausea, dizziness, a tight feeling in the throat or difficulty breathing, the victim needs medical attention right away.

People with known allergies to fire ants may carry a kit for anaphylactic shock which they can administer to prevent a severe reaction.

For most people under most circumstances the stings can be treated by washing the area with soap and water, applying ice, and only check with a doctor if there is severe redness, swelling or itching.

INGESTED POISONS

Symptoms: A victim who has been poisoned may feel nauseated and suffer stomach pains. The victim may vomit and there may be burns around the mouth. Breathing may be abnormal.

If you suspect someone has been poisoned, look for spilled liquids, pill bottles or other evidence that may be useful to medical professionals in identifying the poison and choosing the right treatment.

Swallowed Poisons

Treatment must be immediate: Take any poison containers to a telephone and **call the poison control center at 1-800-222-1222**, 911, or your local emergency response number and carefully follow any instructions you are given.

Treat the victim for shock and monitor their breathing. Save any vomit in a bowl, cook pot or plastic bag to turn over to a health care professional.

Inhaled Poisons

Smoke and certain gasses or fumes are poisonous. A victim of inhaled poisoning may have trouble breathing and may lose consciousness.

Symptoms may include headache, dizziness, and nausea. The victim may lose consciousness without realizing they are in danger.

Treatment must be immediate. Approach the scene carefully to ensure you do not become the next victim. Move the victim to fresh air. Get medical help.

While waiting for help to arrive, regularly check that the victim is still breathing and has a heartbeat. If necessary, perform rescue breathing or CPR.

ELECTRICAL SHOCK

Minor electrical shock is a common household hazard. Fortunately it is usually more surprising than dangerous and does not require medical attention. However, some basic precautions should be taken to insure that the shock does not interfere with the body's normal electrical impulses including the functions of the brain and the heart. Prolonged exposure to a direct source of electricity can also cause severe burns to the skin and the tissue.

In the event of electric shock do NOT rush to assist the victim until you are certain that he is no longer in contact with electricity. Otherwise the current will pass through the victim directly to you.

- If possible, turn off the electricity. If this is not an option, use non-conductive material such as plastic or dry wood to separate the source of electricity from the victim.
- If the injuries appear serious or extensive, dial 9-1-1.
- Check the victim's vital signs such as the depth of his breathing and regularity of his heartbeat. If either one is effected by exposure to electricity or if the victim is unconscious, begin to perform CPR.
- Treat any areas of the victim's body that may have sustained burns.
- If the victim is responsive and

does not appear seriously injured but looks pale or faint, he may be at risk of going into shock. Gently lay him down with his head slightly lower than his chest and his feet elevated.

BRUISES

A typical bruise is caused by traces of blood escaping from small vessels that lie close to the skin's surface. Since our blood vessels become more fragile with age, the elderly tend to bruise easier than healthy adults and children. If a child sustains excessive bruising, it may be an indication of a more serious injury and should be treated accordingly.

If the bruise is on the victim's head, he may have sustained a concussion and should be checked for head trauma.

To reduce the bump and minimize the pain, have the victim elevate the injured area and apply a commercial ice pack or ice cubes wrapped in a towel for 15 to 20 minutes, may repeat every 2-4 hours as needed. Depending on the extent of the injury, this process should be repeated for a few days or until the swelling and the pain begins to dissipate.

DEHYDRATION

There are several ways our body loses water such as sweating, urination, and evaporation as we breathe. Under certain conditions we can give off more water than we take in, and that causes dehydration.

Dehydration is serious and should be treated right away. Symptoms of dehydration include:

- Dark urine or decreased urine production
- Severe thirst
- Tiredness or weakness
- Dry skin and lips
- Decreased sweating
- Loss of appetite, nausea or fainting
- Confusion or dizziness
- Headache, body aches, and muscle cramps

You should protect yourself from dehydration by drinking plenty of fluids before you feel thirsty. Make sure your urine stays clear.

Encourage a victim of dehydration to drink fluids and rest. In hot weather, get the victim to a shady place or into an air-conditioned building or vehicle. Watch the victim until symptoms clear up.

When hiking and camping in remote areas you must

be able to filter your water or chemically decontaminate it.

HEAT INJURIES

Heat Cramps

These cramps are probably related to electrolyte imbalances including sodium, potassium, calcium, and magnesium.

Symptoms of Heat Cramps

Muscle spasms are typically: Painful, Involuntary, Brief, Intermittent, Usually self-limited (go away on their own)

Heat Cramp Treatment

- Heat cramps usually go away whether you do anything or not.
- Resting in a cool place.
- Commercially available electrolyte beverages will provide adequate electrolyte intake.

Heat Exhaustion

Heat exhaustion is caused as the body struggles to keep its internal temperature down. It can be made worse by dehydration.

Symptoms include skin that is pale and clammy from heavy sweating, nausea, and tiredness, dizziness and fainting, headache, muscle cramps, and weakness. It may resemble symptoms of Shock.

Treatment includes having the victim lie down in a cool, shady place with the feet raised. Remove excess clothing. Then cool the victim by applying wet cloths to the body and fanning. If the victim is alert, let him or her sip some water.

Recovery should be quick, but if symptoms remain or progress to fainting, confusion or seizures call 9ll.

Heatstroke

Heat exhaustion, if not treated, can go into heatstroke. The body's cooling system starts to fail and its internal temperature rises to dangerous levels.

Symptoms include skin that is very hot to the touch, is red and either very dry or damp with sweat. The victim may have rapid pulse and rapid, noisy breathing. The victim may be confused and unwilling to cooperate. Ultimately the victim may become unconscious.

Treatment begins with immediately calling for medical assistance. In the meanwhile, move the victim to an air-conditioned or shady area, loosen tight clothing, and cool the skin by fanning and applying wet cloths. If you have ice packs, wrap them in a towel, shirt or other thin barrier and place them under the victim's armpits and against the neck and groin to have the greatest effect. If the victim can drink, give them small amounts of cool water. Keep an eye on the victim's condition and be ready to provide further first aid if necessary.

COLD INJURIES

Frostbite

When skin and tissue get cold enough to freeze, this is frostbite. The injury may hurt or it may be numb.

You can tell when frostbite is beginning as grayish white patches form on the skin. This is a sign that ice crystals are starting to form.

Move the victim into a shelter. If the injury is on an ear or cheek, warm the injury with the exposed palm of your hand. Put a frostbitten hand under clothing against warm skin.

If you suspect that the frostbite is severe, get the victim into dry clothing, wrap the injured area in a blanket, and get the victim to a doctor as soon as possible.

If you are certain the injury will not have a chance to re-freeze,

place it under water that is warm to the touch (not hot!) and watch for normal color to return.

If the injury is on a hand or foot, place dry, sterile gauze between the fingers or toes and cover with a loose bandage.

Hypothermia

When the body's ability to produce heat is overtaken by heat loss, the core temperature will drop. This condition is called hypothermia.

It may happen from not wearing warm enough clothing or wet clothing. The danger is increased by wind, rain, hunger, dehydration, and exhaustion.

Hypothermia can happen when you don't expect it. If you don't have rain gear, a cool, windy shower may chill you. Swimming in cold water or capsizing in cold water may start uncontrollable shivering.

Symptoms include feeling cold or numb, tiredness, inability to think straight, uncontrollable shivering, poor decisions, irritability, stumbling, and loss of consciousness.

Treatment starts with preventing a further drop in temperature. It continues with help in slowly bringing the body temperature back up to normal. You can try any or all of these techniques:

- Move the victim into a shelter. Replace wet clothing with warm, dry clothes. Wrap the victim in a sleeping bag, blankets, jackets or anything handy.
- If conscious and able to swallow, have the victim drink warm liquids.
- Put towels or t-shirts around bottles filled with warm water, then put the bottles in the armpit and groin areas. **Do not attempt to warm arms and legs, this will drive cold blood towards the core.**
- Watch the victim closely for changes in their condition. Call for help.
- Begin CPR if breathing stops or is inadequate.

   Prevention: Wearing Synthetic insulating layers and nylon/Gore-tex outer wear and gloves can protect you from the elements and keep you warm.

THE BEST FIRST AID

The best way to treat injuries is to avoid them. Know and use the safety rules for the activities you do. Look for hazards around your home, school and camp and make sure they are corrected or at least pointed out to others. Safety First—Always!

Portions of this chapter edited and added courtesy of Tim Downs, RN; ACLS, BLS, and First Aid Instructor.

Special thanks to Troop FL-714 for photos

GOALS / NOTES

CHAPTER 7

AQUATICS

Taking a swim on a hot summer day is one of life's great pleasures. Yet there is more to swimming than that—a lot more! Knowing how to stay afloat in water over your head and easily move from place to place makes you—and others around you—safer. It gives you the confidence and self-reliance to participate in water sports where you might end up "in the drink" before you realize what hit you. Think you might enjoy motor boating, water skiing, sailing, or rafting? Does canoeing, kayaking, or snorkeling appeal to you? Then make like an otter and learn to tread water!

Of course, you need to know what you're getting into. Is that water as deep as it looks? What dangerous obstacles may lurk beneath the surface? There is a difference between being brave and being foolhardy, and that difference is in not taking unnecessary risks. A Trailman always follows the Safe Aquatics Method.

SAFE AQUATICS METHOD

All Trail Life USA programs must be conducted using the Safe Aquatics Method:

- All adults and youth who participate in aquatic activities must have a complete and up-to-date health history on file.
- All aquatics activities must have qualified and trustworthy adult supervision.
- Every person must have a buddy with him at all times.
- Areas approved for swimming and water games must be checked for obstacles and segregated into non-swimming (up to chest deep for your shortest non-swimmer) and swimmer area (up to 12 feet deep). An optional beginner area up to around 5-6 feet deep may also be established.
- Only those who have passed their Trail Life USA Swimming Competency test at the Swimmer level may venture into the swimmer area or participate in other aquatics activities.
- All water games and other aquatics activities require a safety orientation and a skill orientation or associated trail badge before participation.
- All aquatics activities other than swimming, water games, snorkeling, and scuba require the wearing of an approved personal flotation device (PFD).
- Proper discipline and adherence to the pool or waterfront rules are required at all times. No horseplay!

Aquatics activities ... require the wearing of an approved personal flotation device (PFD)

RESCUE TECHNIQUES

It is important to learn rescue techniques **before** you need them. You must remain calm and resourceful in order to do any good. From time to time, you hear on the news that someone died trying to save another person from drowning. A Trailman opts for real skill over good intentions and does not waste his good intentions or put himself or others in danger through a poor approach to rescue. While quick action is important, unless you are alone the first thing you should do is check the area to ensure you are safe and send or call someone for help. Then select the method that puts you in the least danger.

Reach - If you can safely reach the victim with an object or part of your body, do it. Many water emergencies take place close to the side of the pool or near the shore. Because you can reach while standing on dry land or in shallow water, this is the most effective method.

Throw - If you cannot reach the victim, can you throw an object that will help him or her float? An object that floats will help. An object with a line attached is best, because you can tow the victim to safety while they hold on.

Row - If you cannot reach or throw, and you have checked for any dangers, the waters are not too rough and you have boating experience, perhaps you can take a boat out to the victim to perform a reach or throw. Make sure to put on a life vest or personal flotation device ("PFD") – you don't want to put yourself in danger also. Don't allow the victim to try and climb into the boat because they might tip you over; just have them hold on while you head back to shore.

Go - If all else fails, you may have to swim out to the victim–preferably "with support," such as a PFD or other flotation device. *Only do this if you are a strong swimmer who is trained in lifesaving techniques.* It is very difficult to swim while helping another person, and someone who is drowning is fighting for their life and may unintentionally pull you under. **NOTE: Many people have died while attempting rescue with this risky method. Use this direct rescue method only in the most urgent of circumstances. The only thing worse than a drowning is a double drowning.**

SWIMMING STROKES

Different strokes allow you to con
centrate on speed or comfort, fun or
survival. Five basic strokes every
Trailman should know are front crawl,
backstroke, sidestroke, breaststroke, and elementary backstroke.

Front Crawl (Freestyle)

The front crawl is a fast and
graceful stroke used in recreational
swimming and racing. The hardest
part to learn is synchronizing your
breathing with the brief moments
your face is above water.

Backstroke

Backstroke is used for recreational swimming and racing rather
than resting or survival. It is fast and
has the advantage that the face
stays out of water. The disadvantage
is poor visibility in your direction of
travel.

Sidestroke

Sidestroke is easy to learn and
is a very restful stroke for long
distance. When done properly
your mouth stays out of water and
you can travel long distances in a
reasonably short period of time.

Breaststroke

It is easy to breathe while using
the breaststroke and you have the
best view of where you are going.
It is not very fast and it is not as
restful as either the side stroke or
the elementary backstroke but it
is a serviceable stroke that gives a
beginning swimmer quick results.

Elementary Backstroke

The elementary backstroke
is an excellent way to cover long
distances with easy breathing, long
restful glides, and an easy transition
to a resting float when you need to
take a break. If you have to return
from a boat ride without the boat,
this stroke is definitely your friend.

FLOATING

Swimming is a strenuous way of
moving from place to place in water.
Floating gives you a chance to stop
and catch your breath. It is an
essential survival skill if you need to
swim further than your endurance
will allow.

You naturally float in water, but
not well enough to breathe. The trick
is to use your buoyancy and balance
to keep your mouth and nose at
the top. When you float properly,
you allow your limbs to rest and
your breathing to slow to normal.
Fortunately, this is an easy skill to
learn, and it could save your life.

WATER SPORTS

Being a swimmer is not merely about swimming. It opens the door to a number of exciting water sports such as rafting, canoeing, motor boating, water skiing, and kayaking.

Canoeing runs the gamut from peaceful early-morning communing with the lake to a heart-racing trip through the rapids.

Sailing—especially if you sail far from shore—is not only exciting, but also offers a historical link to many of the people who colonized America. Though your clothing and equipment may be modern, the feel of the sea beneath your boat, and the unhurried rhythm of open water sailing is the same as that felt by traders, trappers, and pilgrims.

Some people enjoy the rush of a motorboat, whether they are sitting in a chair or standing on a pair of water-skis. Like whitewater rafting or canoeing, raising a wake with a powerboat requires training and concentration to safely enjoy.

Trail badges in these areas begin with passing the Trail Life USA Swimming Competency Test, so make up your mind to do so as soon as possible. Being comfortable in water over your head is one of the most important outdoor skills you can possess.

OUTDOOR SKILLS

CHAPTER

8

NATURE

God made nature and said it was good. He ought to know! Humans made cities, and while they are fine in their own way, they simply can't match the level of artistry and skill you see in a simple forest glade or on a windswept prairie. There are many great lessons about yourself and the world that can only be learned as you get back in touch with the order and pattern of nature.

As a Trailman, you will make some of your best memories in God's great outdoors. Nature is your birthright, but it is equally the birthright of your children and your children's children. Every tree, every flower you see, and every unspoiled view you enjoy is there because the person who came before you did not ruin it. Decide right now not to spoil it for the person who comes along after you. Many people suggest that the only things that you "take with you" are pictures and memories and the only things you leave behind are footprints that are unavoidable.

NATURE IS EVERYWHERE

Nature is everywhere. Even the plastic, metal, and silicon that make up your home computer are made up of elements as old as the earth, sea, and sky. The electricity that powers that computer is akin to the lightning that frightened woolly mammoths and saber tooth cats.

You step closer to nature as it was meant to be when you look at your face in the mirror. Blood runs through you like a restless river, carrying nutrients and oxygen to all points. Your breath comes and goes in an rhythmic tide. Your nervous system, digestion, senses, and muscles work together, each helping the others to make possible the marvelous being you are.

It is when you look out the

window that you take another step toward seeing the big picture. The grass and trees look to the sky for water and sunlight. The birds eat seeds from the holly, and bees forage for nectar from the flowers. The remarkable cooperation that goes on among systems in one body is duplicated in the way living things cooperate in the environment of your own back yard.

Even so, that yard relies on people to look the way it does. If you stopped cutting the grass, trimming the shrubs, and planting

ECOSYSTEMS

A group of plants and animals and the environment in which they live is called an ecosystem. Just as all members of your patrol have different jobs on a campout, every living thing found in a wild area has certain things it takes from the environment and certain things it gives back.

Sunlight helps plants make their own nourishment from the air and ground. Certain animals eat plants and use their stored sunlight and minerals to survive. Other animals

Oikos (home) + logy (study) = Ecology

flowers, it would only take a few years before new trees grew and the yard became a wooded acre. Nature has a built-in order and pattern that has a place for every animal and plant and an animal and plant in every place. Unlike your yard, the woodland glade or open prairie keeps itself looking the way it is supposed to without your mower or hedge clippers doing a thing!

The relationship between different plants and animals, the soil where they stand, and the sky that covers them is both remarkable and beautiful.

eat the plant eaters. The wolf and grizzly bear survive off what is left of the sunlight in the animals they eat. When they die, their minerals go back into the ground where more plants can use them. Sunlight keeps the process going smoothly as long as all the plants, plant eaters, and meat eaters are allowed to do their job.

The story of how animals and plants depend on each other, the weather, sunlight, and water is called **ecology**. Ecology comes from the Greek language. "Oikos" means home and "logy" means study. Ecology is the story of how the family members get along in nature's houses such as deserts, mountains, prairies, forests, and seashores.

....

PLANTS

Plants are the world's oldest users of solar power. They make sugars out of air and water, providing for their own needs and the needs of animals that eat them. They take in carbon dioxide, the waste gas we breathe out, and produce oxygen, the life-sustaining gas we breathe in. They are not only doing this on dry land, but also as microscopic algae thriving in the oceans that cover 7I percent of the Earth's surface.

Not only do plants provide food, they also provide timber, paper, and important medicines. Plants that died long ago provided fossil fuels like oil, coal, and natural gas that release the power of ancient sunlight to power our industry, light our homes, and keep us moving from place to place in speed and comfort.

Plants take in carbon dioxide, the waste gas we breathe out, and produce oxygen, the life-sustaining gas we breathe in.

You should learn to recognize the plants commonly seen in your area. During the growing season, trees can be recognized by their leaves, but even plants that lose their leaves in winter can be identified by their bark, their height, and their overall shape. There are several excellent

books that can help you. Your Troop Leaders may also be of assistance.

WILDLIFE

In the great play of life, plants may be scenery, but animals are the actors that add drama to the wilderness. They play three basic parts: herbivores (plant eaters), carnivores (hunters), and scavengers (those who eat dead animals they find).

You are most likely to see birds, because their ability to fly away from you at a moment's notice gives them confidence around people.

Some animals are rather hard to see because they live underground or in the water or because they hide from you. As your powers of observation increase and you learn to walk quietly and hide carefully, you will have greater success at spotting animals than people who are loud and boisterous.

You can detect many animals that are difficult to see if you know how to look for their signs. Detecting such animals is like detecting the wind: you don't actually see the wind, but you can feel the cool breeze and witness the trees moving. When animals travel through an area they cause a disturbance, too. Tracks left in the mud beside a creek, bird nests, skeletons,

feathers, and even bits of fur left on a barbed wire fence all tell a story to those who will listen.

You should invest in a field guide to animals in your area and see how many creatures you can find.

Getting Along With Wildlife

You are a visitor—animals are residents. Treat their home with respect and behave like a good guest. This includes taking precautions not to disturb animals. You shouldn't closely approach them, handle their nests, or touch and pick them up. Even timid creatures, like mice, will bite if disturbed. Docile appearing animals may have diseases like rabies that affect their natural behavior. But more importantly, you cause the animals stress by intruding in their homes or poking and prodding them. Getting wildlife used to feeding or being handled by humans teaches them undesirable behaviors that can put them—and humans—in danger.

WEATHER

Weather happens because the layer of atmosphere around our planet is constantly changing. The air may move gently in breezes, quickly in gusts, or even violently in tornadoes or hurricanes. It may hold moisture above you in the form of clouds, or that moisture may come down as rain, sleet, or snow. Most remarkable, these weather patterns get their power from sunlight, just as plants do directly and animals do indirectly.

You may hear two words that sound like they mean the same thing, but they are quite different. Weather is the way that clouds, wind, precipitation, and temperature affect you at a given moment. Climate is an overall pattern of weather in an area such as desert, temperate, or rain forest. A rainstorm in Topeka, Kansas, is weather, but icy winds at the South Pole are a consistent part of the Antarctic climate.

There are certain things climate can tell you when you are dressing for an outdoor activity, but you especially need to be aware of the weather as time for a campout approaches. Some of your hiking essentials, such as rain gear, remind you that even the best weather reports can very quickly change.

WEATHER

is the way that clouds, wind, precipitation, and temperature affect you at a given moment.

CLIMATE

is an overall pattern of weather in an area such as desert, temperate, or rain forest.

GOOD STEWARDSHIP

Left to itself, nature usually maintains a smooth balance that gives opportunities for many different plants and animals to live together.

Unfortunately, sometimes the activities of man disrupt the delicate balance over large areas. In some places, the natural order is very hard to see, and it is highly unlikely there will ever be cougars or bison in New York's Central Park again. That makes treating areas where nature still has a significant presence all the more important.

There are some laws which protect habitat from wildfire and guard animals from wanton slaughter. In National Parks, it is illegal to remove any natural object—even a small pebble—from your campsite.

A Trailman does not have to be threatened by fines or imprisonment to treat nature with respect. When you love something, and when you live the Trailman Motto to "Walk Worthy," this all makes perfect sense and you will protect nature. When we recite the Trailman's Oath, part of it says that we will "do our best to...be a good steward of creation."

LOW IMPACT CAMPING

There are more people on Earth than there were a century ago, but we still have to operate in the same amount of room. That makes caring wisely for the wild areas we have left all the more important.

There are a few simple things Trailmen can do to walk more softly in the wilderness while still having a great time. If you remember from the last chapter, deserts, mountains, prairies, and forests are homes. Just as you would take off muddy boots before entering your house, taking similar precautions in nature's houses will become a habit that demonstrates respect for God's creation.

Prepare in Advance

Know what you will need to bring, what you should leave at home, what you should do, and what you should avoid doing. The best way to do this is to ask the land manager for suggestions.

No Trailblazing

It may require walking a few extra steps, but stay on the prepared paths and camp whenever possible in prepared campgrounds. These places were reserved for human wear and tear so that the surrounding areas could remain pristine for future visitors. Remember, when you blaze a new trail, other people will be tempted to use it after you.

Not all wild areas are as durable as the grass in your yard. Some delicate places will hold the scars of your passing for a long time.

Leave it Intact

If it belongs there, it stays there. If it doesn't belong there, pack it

out. In National Parks and Monuments, removing natural objects is a violation of the Antiquities Act.

Even if it's not illegal, it is unethical to collect "souvenirs" of your visit that deprive future visitors the same experiences you enjoyed. Don't dam creeks, dig trenches, or leave trash. Don't leave "pioneering" projects, such as camp gadgets, behind.

Take nothing but pictures, leave nothing but footprints, and make nothing but memories.

Be Careful With Fire

Campfires have their place in the outdoors, and that place is a carefully prepared area set aside by the land manager. Consider using a camping stove if your aim is to heat water or cook food.

If you are camping in a prepared place with a fire ring, use the existing spot rather than building a fire in a new place.

If you do use fire, make sure the area around it is clear of twigs, branches, and anything that can catch fire; and always watch a fire carefully to prevent flames from spreading to the surroundings. It only takes a moment to start, but it may take years for nature to heal from it.

Remember never to run or horseplay around an open fire. A tragedy could occur if a Trailman were to trip or fall into a fire or onto hot coals.

Wise Sanitation

Water you use at home is treated before being released. Obviously, you can't return water to its source as clean as you got it, but you can take precautions to minimize your impact on the land.

For short stays, remove solids from dishwater and put them in the trash. Then take dishwater or rinse water at least 200 feet (75 steps) from open water and fling it out rather than pouring it in one spot. For longer stays, dig a sump hole. It should be about a foot across and two feet deep. Remove solids from dishwater before emptying it. Fill in the sump hole before you leave, and return the land to a natural appearance. Water used to wash your body should be treated with the same precautions as dishwater.

It is less adventurous but a lot more pleasant to use restroom facilities at campgrounds. If you must dig a cathole for human waste, it should be located at least 200 feet (about 75 steps) from open water, trails or campsites. Dig a hole about 7 inches deep. After using it, fill it in with the soil you dug. Leave the area as close to its original appearance as possible, but leave a stick in the ground to warn people against using the same spot. Sanitize your hands.

For longer stays with several people, dig a latrine. A latrine is a shallow trench about four feet long and seven inches deep. After each use, sprinkle a layer of dirt to abate odors and keep away flies. Return the area to a natural appearance before moving on.

Getting Along With Other Visitors

One of the greatest parts about camping is getting away from it all. Select your campsite in a way to protect your own privacy and the privacy of others. Do not make excessive noise or use brightly colored tents. Leave loud electronics behind. Make sure you do not enter another campsite without asking permission.

CHAPTER

9

HIKING

Some forms of travel are nothing but moving from place to place. When you get out of a vehicle and actually put boots on the ground, you connect to your surroundings each step of the journey with a thousand sights, sounds, and smells. Unlike the motorist whizzing by, you are not just on the landscape, you are in it. You are a part of what is going on. If something catches your eye, you can pause for a moment to take a closer look. Hiking is great when you have the right equipment, possess the right skills, and keep yourself in good shape. Some people think they won't enjoy hiking, and there is usually a story behind that. Perhaps you are one of those people. If you have had a bad experience hitting the trail, go have a good experience to put it into perspective. Let's show you how.

BASIC ESSENTIALS

You wouldn't take a drive without bringing a jack and a spare tire. You shouldn't take a hike without the basic essentials.

The basic essentials for a day hike balance comfort and safety against keeping your day pack light to carry.

- Pocketknife
- First-Aid Kit
- Extra Clothing
- Water Bottle
- Trail Food
- Matches and Fire Starters
- Hat
- Sun Protection and Rain Gear
- Flashlight
- Map and Compass
- Trailman's Standard or Hiking Staff
- Emergency Contact Information

FOOD

Food carried on a day hike should be simple to prepare and easy to eat. It should be able to survive several hours in a pack without refrigeration.

A hearty breakfast before you begin will serve as a good foundation for an active day. Sandwiches are great because they don't create a mess—you can hold them in one hand and eat everything but the wrapper. You will also want to carry fruit, nuts, and raisins for quick energy and flavor.

Candy bars such as those found in a vending machine are empty calories, and they may melt when warmed by the sun. Special energy bars sold for hikers do much better on the trail. Cheese, jerky, and peanut butter on crackers work very well. All of these foods have two things in common: no dirty dishes and no soiled utensils. The key to good grub on the trail is to live simply and well.

DRINKING WATER

Up to 60% of your body is made up of water. Keeping properly hydrated is more important than avoiding thirst—it is literally a matter of personal safety. Whether it's hot or cold out, drink at least 8 cups of water a day. In hotter weather, you'll need more water to replace

favorite flavor packets. That has the added effect of encouraging you to drink more water more often.

TRIP/ACTIVITY PLAN

A well-planned trip/activity is a safe and comfortable trip/activity. It is especially important to leave written and clear expectations of when you are leaving along with your contact information. Include where you are going and when you plan to return. That way if you encounter difficulties, people will know how to help you. Make sure

fluids lost through perspiration. If you're drinking enough, you'll have clear urine. If your urine is yellow, increase your intake of water. Remember, you should be drinking water *before* you feel thirsty.

Water should come from a trusted source. Water from public utilities is usually safe to drink as-is. Water from natural sources such as lakes or rivers may give you diseases or parasites.

You can make natural water safe for drinking by boiling it for a full minute, using filters designed for backpackers, or treating the water with purifying tablets. Since tablets give the water a slightly unpleasant flavor, you might want to bring your

Make sure your trip plan contains **the five W's: where** you are going, **when** you will depart and return, **who** is going with you, **why** you are going, **what** you are taking, and **how** you can be contacted in case of an emergency. **This information should be left with parents and other leaders.**

your trip plan contains the five W's: **where** you are going, **when** you will depart and return, **who** is going with you, **why** you are going, **what** you are taking, and how you can be contacted in case of an emergency. This information should be left with parents and other leaders.

OUTDOOR CLOTHING

Temperatures inside your clothing change as your body gets a good workout and as the outdoor temperature changes over the course of a day. How you feel one moment is not how you may feel in a few minutes or a few hours. The answer is simple: dress in layers. If you can put more clothing on or take some clothing off, you can stay in your comfort zone.

Choose your clothing wisely. If you prefer natural fibers, wool keeps up to 70% of its ability to hold warmth when wet. It can be itchy, so wear it over a t-shirt. On the other hand, cotton loses its ability to insulate you when moist, and it dries much more slowly than wool. Syn-

thetics can be both comfortable and warm whether you stay wet or dry.

Raingear is not a luxury—it's a necessity. If you plan to do a lot of outdoor adventuring, get the best rain gear you can afford. Modern materials allow air through the fabric without passing moisture. This keeps you from getting wet with your own perspiration.

A hat will help protect you from both rain and from sun – when made of the right fabric, it can keep you warm during the winter, and can keep you cool during the summer.

Footgear

You may survive an hour of church in pinching black dress shoes, but you won't last long on the trail where every step involves resting your weight plus the weight of your gear on each foot. Your footgear should fit well and be "broken in" to the shape of your feet before you need it for a day hike.

Hiking shoes may be fine for easy trails or pavement. For more rugged terrain or winter outings, hiking boots will give you the support and protection you need.

Keeping your feet dry is essential. Wise hikers wear hiking socks that cushion the feet over a pair of polypropylene sock liners that wick moisture from the skin, reduce friction, and help prevent blisters. A change of socks on the trail can be a vacation for your feet, especially if your socks get wet. Remember that if your feet are miserable, the rest of you will be miserable as well. Cotton socks are not a good idea, wool or synthetics that wick away moisture are always best.

PACE

It is unkind and unsafe to put the fastest hikers up front. It causes serious morale problems with the slower people struggling to keep up and increases the likelihood of them losing sight of the group and getting lost. If you put the slowest people up front, the problem takes care of itself. Remember, everyone must finish the hike before the hike is over—so you aren't saving time by running on ahead.

Occasional breaks keep you fresher. Turning recreation into drudgery defeats

the whole purpose of a troop hike. You should plan your trip to allow rests of five minutes every half hour to make grabbing a quick bite or taking on water more comfortable and less disruptive.

> Everyone must finish the hike before the hike is over—so you aren't saving time by running on ahead.

ABILITY

Trails come in all shapes and sizes. Steep and rugged terrain should be reserved for more experienced hikers in good physical shape. Your troop may want to plan two activities on the same outing to give less experienced boys an alternative. You are not doing a boy a favor by encouraging him to take a hike above his ability. You are not doing yourself a favor, either, which you'll realize as you help him carry out his gear in addition to your own. If you run the new guy ragged on a mountain path, you'll lose a hiking buddy forever. You should start off with shorter hikes to build endurance and skill before striking out on a longer trek.

HIKING SAFELY

The trail is no place to take unnecessary chances—that is, unless you don't mind being carried out or carrying out one of your buddies. Be careful where you put your feet, how you cross moving water, and what you climb upon.

When walking along a roadway, use the sidewalk if there is one. Otherwise walk in single file on the left side, facing the traffic. Hiking at night is strongly discouraged; but if you find yourself having to hike after sunset, wear light-colored clothes or use flashlights or reflective armbands to alert others to your presence. Do not insist on the right of way—you could end up dead right.

Railway right-of-ways are owned by the railroads. Unless marked otherwise, they consider walking on or beside tracks trespassing on their private property; and if they are still in use, this is very dangerous and should be avoided.

Trail Life Standard (hiking staff)

The use of your Trail Life Standard as a hiking staff can be extremely helpful. Not only can it help to steady you if the footing gets a little unsteady, but it can be used to push aside branches, serve as an emergency lever, first aid splint or fishing pole, poke behind rocks, test how deep a "puddle" on the trail might be before you wade through it, and even as part of a tripod or an emergency shelter.

INCLEMENT WEATHER

Always check the weather forecast before you leave for an outing to help you decide what to wear, what to bring, and whether or not to reschedule.

People are killed or severely injured every year by lightning strikes. If you are caught out during a lightning storm, take cover if possible, otherwise avoid open meadows, ridge tops, and tall or solitary trees where you or an object near you is a tempting target for lightning bolts. Stay away from metallic objects, including fences and tent poles. If you are in a building, do not use the electricity or any landline telephones unless it is an emergency.

Tornadoes don't mess around. Their winds travel over 100 miles per hour, throw debris— including you— around, uproot trees, and flatten houses. If you are caught out in the path of a tornado and you cannot find more substantial shelter, find a low-lying spot, such as a ditch, and lie there with your arms over your head to protect it. Do not expect to find shelter beneath a bridge. Never seek shelter in a mobile home, car, or trailer. These are liable to be sent flying with you trapped inside.

NAVIGATION

Finding your way in the outdoors is a test, but you have lots of friends trying to give you the answers.

The rising sun says, "Hey, east is over here!" As it moves through the sky, it even gives you the time of day. "This is north!" says the star Polaris. Even when the sky is overcast, lines of force streaming down to you from the north magnetic pole are talking to your compass. If that isn't enough, there are all sorts of distinctive landmarks that practically shout, "Remember me? I'm that mark on your map!"

Once you start noticing these things, it's hard not to see them, especially if you are wise enough to remember your map and compass. And using these skills to find your way off-road gives you a wonderful feeling of confidence and independence and of being at home in God's creation.

Reading a map is a lot like reading a book. You have to speak the language. Fortunately, the language of maps is made up of a relatively small set of symbols and colors, and you don't have to worry about grammar and spelling! Learning to read the compass is even faster.

A map and compass also has the advantage of never running out of power because of dead batteries!!!

Topographic Maps

These versatile maps are made by the United States Geological Survey (USGS); together, they cover the entire United States. You sometimes hear them called quadrangle maps because they show a square area. They are perfect for hiking, because they show things that are important if you are travelling cross country. In addition to roads and cities, they include obstacles like swamps, rivers, and mountain ranges, and they indicate the steepness of the land by contour lines.

You can purchase maps from the USGS website www.usgs.gov or by calling I-800-HELP-MAP. You can also order them by mail from:

U.S. Geological Survey
Distribution Branch
Box 25286
Federal Center
Denver, CO 80225

Map Symbols

A topographic map is different from an aerial photograph in two very important ways. First, it cuts down on distracting details that do not help you find your way.

Second, it includes a lot of extra information such as contour lines that give you more of a feel for the shape of a land than you get from a photo taken straight down.

Marginal Notes

Some very important information can be found around the edge of the map in places where the shape of the land is not drawn. *North* is usually the top of the map and *south* is usually the bottom. That, of course,

makes the left side *west* and the right side *east*. You will find a *true north arrow* on the map's declination diagram, which shows the difference between the *magnetic north pole* in Northern Canada and true north, the actual point around which the Earth revolves. The amount of declination varies over time because the magnetic north pole moves over time. At this writing, a line near the Mississippi River intersects both the magnetic and true north poles. On this line, your compass will point at true north. East of this line, your compass will point west of true north, and west of it your compass will point to the more eastward. The current magnetic declination in the United States varies from 18

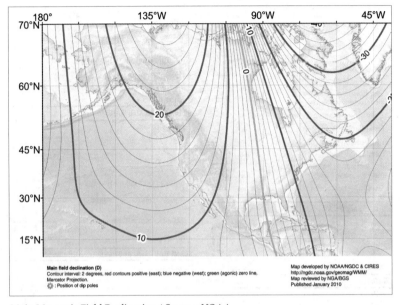

Main Magnetic Field Declination / Source: NOAA

degrees west in Maine to 22 degrees east in Alaska. Depending on where you hike, magnetic declination can cause a considerable error if not corrected. Correction of declination is presented in the compass section.

Another important piece of information is the date the map was made. Buildings come and go, roads change course, and even something as important as a reservoir may appear or disappear.

Certain maps represent unique situations with non-standard symbols. These symbols will be described in the marginal notes.

The scale of the map and the contour interval are needed to give you an idea of the horizontal and vertical distances you will travel. Both are important, especially if you are worried about the ruggedness of your hike.

Charts of Map Symbols

The following charts were provided by the US Geological Survey. In your hiking trips, you will probably use a small fraction of these symbols.

BOUNDARIES

National	
State or territorial	
County or equivalent	
Civil township or equivalent	
Incorporated city or equivalent	
Federally administered park, reservation, or monument (external)	
Federally administered park, reservation, or monument (internal)	
State forest, park, reservation, or monument and large county park	
Forest Service administrative area*	
Forest Service ranger district*	
National Forest System land status, Forest Service lands*	
National Forest System land status, non-Forest Service lands*	
Small park (county or city)	

BUILDINGS AND RELATED FEATURES

Building	
School; house of worship	
Athletic field	
Built-up area	

CONTOURS

Topographic

Index	6000
Approximate or indefinite	
Intermediate	
Approximate or indefinite	
Supplementary	
Depression	

RAILROADS AND RELATED FEATURES

Standard guage railroad, single track	
Standard guage railroad, multiple track	
Narrow guage railroad, single track	
Narrow guage railroad, multiple track	

RIVERS, LAKES, AND CANALS

Perennial stream	
Perennial river	
Intermittent stream	
Intermittent river	
Disappearing stream	
Falls, small	
Falls, large	
Rapids, small	
Rapids, large	

RIVERS, LAKES, AND CANALS – *continued*

Perennial lake/pond	
Intermittent lake/pond	
Dry lake/pond	*Dry Lake*
Narrow wash	
Wide wash	*Wash*
Canal, flume, or aqueduct with lock	
Elevated aqueduct, flume, or conduit	
Aqueduct tunnel	
Water well, geyser, fumarole, or mud pot	o o
Spring or seep	*

ROADS AND RELATED FEATURES

Primary highway	
Secondary highway	
Light duty road	
Unimproved road	
Trail	
Highway or road with median strip	
Highway or road under construction	*Under Const*
Highway or road underpass; overpass	
Highway or road tunnel	

SUBMERGED AREAS AND BOGS

Marsh or swamp	
Submerged marsh or swamp	
Wooded marsh or swamp	
Submerged wooded marsh or swamp	

SURFACE FEATURES

Levee	*Levee*
Sand or mud	*Sand*
Disturbed surface	
Gravel beach or glacial moraine	*Gravel*
Tailings pond	*Tailings Pond*

TRANSMISSION LINES AND PIPELINES

Power transmission line; pole; tower	
Telephone line	*Telephone*
Aboveground pipeline	
Underground pipeline	*Pipeline*

VEGETATION

Woodland	
Shrubland	
Orchard	

Using Contour Lines

Contour lines allow you to see the rise and fall of the land on a flat map. They actually give you more information than you could see on an aerial photo.

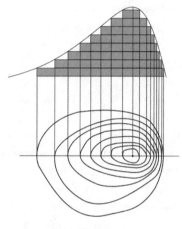

Each line represents an equal change in altitude, and it makes sense that closely spaced lines represent steep terrain while widely spaced lines represent a gradual slope. The amount of altitude, called the contour interval, is marked on the map. It usually equals I, 5, I0, 20, 40, or 80 feet. These wide differences are meant to give you the most meaningful information without overwhelming you. For plains, a smaller contour interval of five feet gives you more detail, while mountains would require a much larger interval to avoid using thousands

of tightly packed contour lines.

Computer Assisted Routes

If you are planning to hike or bike along roadways, you may want to use one of many mapping websites to assist you. These give you clear instructions and the ability to print your results with both map and written directions, and they may even help you locate points of interest. You have to be careful when planning a hike or biking trip versus a car trip since these programs tend to favor highway travel by default. Select the "avoid highways" option or learn how to "choose alternate route."

Try *www.mapquest.com* or *maps.google.com*

The Orienteering Compass

There are many types of compass on the market today. Chances are, you'll get the most use out of yours with the least work if you own an orienteering (base plate) compass.

Every compass works by a magnetized rotating needle that aligns itself with the earth's magnetic field so that the red end of the needle points toward the magnetic north pole.

In the orienteering compass pictured to the the next page, the compass housing is mounted on

a base plate. The base plate has a *direction of travel arrow* used to take and follow compass bearings. Inside the housing is a block arrow with a red half indicating north. This is called the orienting arrow. The parallel lines next to the *orienting arrow* are the compass longitude (north-south) lines.

Correcting for Magnetic Declination

The three magnetic declination correction methods mentioned here make both the compass and map bearings agree with either true north or magnetic north. In each method you will need to look up the magnetic declination for the area of travel either on a recent map or on the Internet.

Method I: Draw magnetic north lines on the map. This method is preferred for the sport of orienteering. It is the easiest to use because the map has magnetic north lines drawn on it. The downside is that magnetic north changes over time and these maps have to be updated periodically. Although the map declination diagram can be used to draw magnetic north lines, this is not recommended due to its limited accuracy and the drift of magnetic north over time.

A good method is to look up the current declination adjustment online, set your compass (or use a protractor) to make a series of parallel starter lines at the map vertical and horizontal edges and then draw the lines using a yardstick or other long straight edge. Note that the left and right edges of the map represent lines of longitude (true north-south lines) and the top and bottom edges of the map represent lines of latitude (true east-west lines).

Method 2: Use a compass with an

adjustment for magnetic declination. This method is easier to set up and use with old maps. All you have to do is set the compass adjustment for the current magnetic declination. For west declination of X degrees, adjust the orienting arrow to the west X degrees to the compass bearing (360 – X). For east declination of Y degrees, adjust the orienting arrow to the east Y degrees to the compass bearing (Y). Then use the compass longitude lines to align with the longitude (true north-south) lines on the map. Generally, you will need to add true north lines parallel to the map vertical edges on your map for this method, but as magnetic north moves, you will only need change the declination adjustment on the compass.

Method 3: Manually make adjustment for magnetic declination between map (true north) and compass bearings. This method is the hardest to use but works with any old compass and map.

To adjust a map bearing to a compass bearing, add the value for west declination and subtract the value for east declination.

To adjust a compass bearing to a map bearing, add the value for east declination and subtract for west declination.

Map and Compass Techniques

In these descriptions, it is assumed that either magnetic declination correction method 1 or 2 is used so the map and compass bearings agree. If method 3 is used, you will need to make the manual adjustments for using compass bearings on the map and using map bearings with the compass.

To find a bearing on a map and then follow it, **first** place your compass on the area map with the base plate edge connecting where you are to where you want to go. **Second,** set the compass heading by turning the compass dial until the compass longitude lines align with the map north lines. **Third,** remove the compass from the map and hold it level in front of you with the direction of travel arrow pointing straight ahead. Turn your body

until the red end of the needle is directly over the orienting arrow, pointing to the "N" on the dial. The direction of travel arrow now points precisely to your destination. Look up, sight on a landmark and walk to it. Repeat this procedure until you reach your destination.

When you see a feature and you want to locate it on the map, **first** take a bearing to that feature, then place the compass on the map with the base plate edge lined up with your location. **Second,** rotate the entire compass on the map around your location until the compass longitude lines align with the map north lines. **Third,** look along the edge of the base plate for the topographic feature you saw.

To determine where you are on a topographic map, you need to pick out two known features, such as mountain peaks. For each feature, take a compass bearing

to the feature. Place the compass on the map with the feature at the edge of the base plate. Rotate the compass around the feature until the compass longitude lines align with the map north lines. Then draw a line along the edge of the base plate and through the feature. After you do two features, the intersection of the two lines is your approximate location. For best accuracy, use features with bearings at roughly a right angle.

If you are on a trail marked on a map, progress can be checked with a bearing measurement to a single feature off to the side of the trail. Then the intersection of the bearing to the feature and the trail is your location.

Using a GPS Receiver

Affordable, hand-held GPS (Global Positioning System) receivers have revolutionized the art of navigation. You may use one for

simple navigation, mapping, or for the exciting sport of geocaching.

You should not have a GPS receiver as your sole means of finding your way home, because anything that interrupts the signal, a loss of battery power, or a simple malfunction could leave you utterly stranded.

Knowing how to use GPS does not substitute for the skill of using map and compass. Some of the times when it is most urgent to know where you are and where you're going, you are likely not to have your trusty (and costly) device at hand.

GPS receivers give readings in hours, minutes, and seconds of latitude and longitude. You should know how to find your position on a map using these numbers to get good use out of one.

GEOCACHING

As you become more confident with navigating by map, compass, and GPS, you may want to try your hand at geocaching. This modern sport involves finding hidden waterproof containers called "caches;" each cache includes a logbook that you can sign and date. Some of the larger caches may contain items for trading. Remember your manners and leave behind something of equal value.

There are lists of geocaching caches on the internet and clubs to help you enjoy this hobby. You do need to mix your enthusiasm with a good dose of common sense: never go out looking by yourself, and never cross private property without getting permission.

LOST ... AND FOUND

Good preparation before you go on your hike will help you avoid being lost. If you do get "turned around," don't make it harder on people trying to help you by wandering around in a panic.

Stop: Being unsure where you are is not the end of the world. Drink some water and eat something. Get comfortable and relax.

Think: Perhaps you can think your way out of the situation by looking at the map and trying to retrace your steps or seeing where you may have taken the wrong route.

Look: Look for your tracks in mud or snow. Look for landmarks and listen for your companions.

React: If you think you know where you are, cautiously proceed to get back on track. Otherwise, stay where you are and wait to be found. In a worst case scenario, you can survive for several days without water and several weeks without food. If you stay on the move, you will venture into places that have already been searched. It is much better to keep your head than to lose your cool. Find shelter, light a fire, say a prayer, and exercise patience. This is the time to use the emergency contact information referenced on your list of essentials – if you have a cell phone with you, call – otherwise knowing who else might be in the area who can help you can help you think of other possible answers.

HIKER'S CODE

Hiking is fun except when it's not. The quickest way to spoil everyone's fun is to make easily avoidable mistakes.

HIKER'S CODE*

You are responsible for yourself, so be prepared:

- **With knowledge and gear.** Become self-reliant by learning about the terrain, conditions, local weather, and your equipment before you start.
- **To leave your plans.** Tell someone where you are going, the trails you are hiking, when you will return, and your emergency plans.
- **To stay together.** When you start as a group, hike as a group and end as a group. Pace your hike to the slowest person.
- **To turn back.** Weather changes quickly. Fatigue and unexpected conditions can also affect your hike. Know your limitations and when to postpone your hike.
- **For emergencies.** Even if you are headed out for just an hour, an injury, severe weather, or a wrong turn could become life-threatening. Don't assume you will be rescued; know how to rescue yourself.
- **To share the Hiker's Code with others.**

*Developed and endorsed by the White Mountain National Forest and New Hampshire Fish and Game.

CHAPTER
10

CAMPING

It's late. Your Trailmaster told you it's almost time for lights out. You move your folding camp chair from its place near the campfire and store it under the dining fly. It's just a little chilly as the autumn stars come out. That's okay. You go into your tent, quickly shuck out of your uniform, and get into your sleeping bag and zip it up. The warmth returns, and all is comfortable again. It's much like being in bed at home, yet you don't hear traffic noises or the television downstairs. Instead, you hear the croaking of frogs, the preparations of your fellow campers, and the soft rustle of grass beneath your tent floor as you turn over on your side. Life is good.

Camping is fun in general. It's a lot more fun when it's the end result of proper equipment and good planning. The skills that cinched getting Ready Trailman rank for you are keeping you safe, happy, and comfortable.

BASIC SKILLS CAMPOUTS

A simple "overnighter" is a great way to get your camping legs. You can bring your equipment in the trunk of your car and practice setting up your tent or dining fly, cooking meals, cleaning up, and learning how to lay out a sleeping bag on level ground free of rocks and sticks for a comfortable, uninterrupted night's sleep.

PLANNING A CAMPING TRIP

If you are planning a trip with your troop, menus and duty rosters should be drawn up in advance. Use the menus to plan your grocery run and help decide how much the outing will cost each boy. Resolve to live simply and well by taking only the equipment and personal extras you actually need. A good plan also includes keeping an eye on the weather report.

BACKPACKING

Backpacking trips are some of the most exciting adventures that await you. Knowing what to bring and how to prepare yourself is a skill you will need to learn from your Troop Leaders before you head out. Even your choice of backpack style and size depends on your personal build and your goals.

Resolve to live simply and well by taking only the equipment and personal extras you actually need.

morning if you have to lay on it. Likewise, small branches become logs.

To pitch your tent, spread out your ground cloth and unpack your tent on top of it. Your ground cloth should be slightly smaller than the tent itself. If it is larger, fold it under so that nothing sticks out. Otherwise, you'll find it has a natural talent for channeling rainwater under the tent so that you and your belongings get an unwanted soaking!

Even if it does not rain, tents tend to get wet with dew. You need to let the tent dry out as much as possible before you pack it. Clean off leaves or grass. You may not be able to dry the tent completely before you leave the camp, but you should dry it as soon as you return from your trip by hanging it on the clothesline or setting it up in the sunlight.

While modern tents tend to be treated to reduce the effect of invisible UV rays, you will lengthen the life of your tent if you pack it up while not in use.

There are several styles of tents to choose from; more experienced boys or your Troop Leaders can help you quickly come up to speed and choose a tent appropriate for you and for your troop's camping habits.

PITCHING A TENT

Selecting where to set up camp will make a big difference in how much you enjoy your camping experience. Your Troop Leaders and patrol can teach you plenty of things about safe places to pitch your tent. Make sure you keep a teachable attitude and you will avoid a lot of uncomfortable situations!

You should put your tent on a level surface. Leave natural ground cover intact, but set sticks and rocks aside to be replaced when you leave. Remember that a small rock will become a giant boulder by

NO FLAMES IN TENTS

It can't be stressed enough … no sources of open flame in tents; no heaters, no lanterns, no candles—no kidding! For lighting, use one of the many safe, battery-powered lights available where camping equipment is sold. Tents protect you from wind and rain but they are not designed to retain heat. You keep yourself warm through proper attire and an appropriately rated sleeping bag. Even tents that are rated flame resistant will burn under the right conditions.

SLEEPING ARRANGEMENTS

Sleeping bags are rated for different temperatures. Buying the warmest bag is not always wise—something you might discover in late spring when it's too cold to sleep on top of it but too warm to sleep in it. To some degree, you can keep from roasting in an over-warm

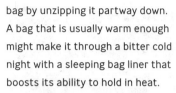

bag by unzipping it partway down. A bag that is usually warm enough might make it through a bitter cold night with a sleeping bag liner that boosts its ability to hold in heat.

A sleeping pad under your sleeping bag will increase your comfort by adding softness and preventing the ground from absorbing your heat. Make sure you sleep on a level surface. If you cannot be completely level, place the bag so that your head is uphill.

You lose a lot of heat through your head and feet in cold weather. This is just as true in a tent as in the open air. Wear a stocking cap or beanie and clean dry socks as you sleep in your bag, and you will feel much warmer.

Have a safe place for items such as your prescription glasses, your watch, or your wallet. Many people use one of their shoes or boots for this. Many tents have a net pocket you may also use.

Do not sleep in your uniform. While it may be cold when you first get into your tent, brave the chill of taking off the shirt, pants, and shoes, and you'll sleep better. You'll also wake up without sweat-soaked clothes in the morning cold. Some savvy campers remain in their sleeping bag while slipping on their pants and pulling the shirt around. This allows you to use heat remaining in the bag to warm your clothes. When camping with your Troop, remember that Navigators should only tent with other Navigators. Same for Adventurers, they only tent with other Adventurers. Exceptions can be made for brothers. An adult should not be sharing a tent with a boy unless the adult is the parent of the boy.

KEEPING CLEAN

Just because Mom and Dad are not watching you is no reason to let your personal hygiene suffer. If you do not keep yourself and your camp food clean, you may be in for a very unpleasant experience.

Wash before meals, after using the bathroom, and before preparing food to avoid spreading germs. If there is no way to bathe, consider taking a few pre-moistened wipes or "towelettes" in a moisture proof container and place a no-rinse hand sanitizer by food preparation stations and latrines. Pre-moistened wipes are especially good for backpacking.

Part of keeping clean is common sense. It may not be as obvious, but wearing clean clothes is a very

important part of your personal hygiene. This is especially true about socks and underwear.

When you bring soap, consider bringing a small bar—like you see in public places—rather than a full-sized bath bar. There are even specially made soaps for camping. Your towel and facecloth will look clean longer if they are a dark color rather than pure white. Hang them up to dry after each use.

LEAVE IT AS YOU FOUND IT

Great care should be used to leave the campsite as good—or better—than you found it. Pack out what you packed in, and if other campers before you were less considerate, correct their mistakes.

Form a line and cross the ground at least twice, removing everything that does not belong there. You did not complain when you dropped the item, so you should not complain when you have to pick it up.

A Trailman is a good steward of God's great outdoors. He treats the land with respect. Not only is it the right thing to do, it also increases your chances of being asked to come back.

WOODS TOOLS SAFETY RULES

Never use a knife or any woods tools without being properly trained. Knives and woods tools are great to have, but they are dangerous in the hands of an untrained boy. Make sure you get permission and are trained properly and that you insist on your friends being safe, too.

Rule	Knife	Saw	Ax
Covering blade when not in use	Close safely (fingers away from blade)	Blade sheathed	Blade sheathed
Carrying	Carry with blade closed	Carry with blade sheathed	Carry with head down and blade sheathed
Passing	Pass with blade closed	Pass with blade turned away	Pass with head down and blade turned away
Safety region	Safety circle (no one within arm's length)	Safety circle (no one within arm's length)	Ax yard 10' in diameter with no overhanging obstructions
When using	Cut away from yourself	Hold log on single chopping block and saw on the other side of the block	Chop/split logs on a chopping block
Use protective gear	Safety glasses recommended	Work gloves and safety glasses	Heavy boots, long pants, work gloves, and safety glasses
To sharpen	Whetstone or diamond stone - push blade away on stone at a 30-degree angle	Replace blade	Use file on secured ax head

Keep your woods tools sharp and do not use if dull, damaged, or loose. Never throw, strike with another tool, or misuse any woods tool.

COOKING

Cooking is one of the most important skills to have for long term camping. A good hot breakfast gets a frosty winter morn off to a rousing start. When you're tired after a long hike or a day of outdoor activity, you will have worked up a good hunger and you need an equally good meal to satisfy it.

FOOD ON A CAMPOUT

> *No one was born a great cook; one learns by doing.*
>
> **JULIA CHILD**

Hot or Cold?

To some degree your choice of hot or cold depends on the climate. If it is cold outside, a hot drink gives you valuable warmth. In hot weather there are few things as refreshing as a nice cold drink. Where solid food is concerned, the matter becomes much simpler. What you eat at the start and end of a busy day should be substantial, and there should be at least one hot item, whether it is toast, flapjacks or oatmeal with breakfast or a nice stew with dinner. Lunch will most likely come during a break between activities and it should be simple to prepare and quick to clean up. Hand or finger foods like a ham sandwich are quick to prepare, provide nutrition, are easy to clean up after, and will satisfy you quickly and get you back in the action.

Cooking Flames

There are basically three ways to cook outdoors, each with their advantages and disadvantages.

For stationary camps, you may

want to use **propane stoves** under a dining fly. They are as close to an outdoor kitchen as you'll find. Propane stoves light instantly with a single match or fire starter and they come to full heat at once, offering you fine control over the height of the flame. They also have the benefit of not requiring you to gather and prepare firewood on a rainy day.

You may opt for the challenge and adventure of **lighting a campfire** yourself to cook dinner. That opens a whole host of issues such as properly preparing the ground, knowing whether open flames are even permitted in your area, and knowing how to do a proper fire lay.

In a pinch, you can start a campfire most anywhere so knowing how to light and control a wood fire is a valuable skill. However it is best not to rely on this method when you are going to be tired, need to have quick results, or the weather is not willing to cooperate.

Ultralight stoves are good for boiling water on a backpacking trip. They don't take up much room, and for light duty jobs such as heating water for backpacking food, they really fill the bill. These stoves are only really useful for preparing individual portions.

Propane stove

Ultralight stove

Living Simply and Well

Unless you really enjoy cleanup duty and you have unlimited space in the vans or troop trailer, give some serious thought on ways you can prepare wholesome, enticing meals with fewer materials.

A spork (spoon with serrated fork end) takes the place of two utensils. Dehydrated meals eaten in their own bag mean fewer dishes. Frankly, some menu items are quite messy to prepare, which is why there are several good standbys you see experienced campers use on trip after trip. Dutch oven cobblers, one-eyed jacks, flapjacks, bacon, French toast, and hobo meals are simple meals that require a minimum of muss and fuss to make, eat, and clean up.

Just as you can save room in your grooming supplies by bringing a small bar of hand soap rather than a full bath-sized bar, you can also trim down on your cooking materials by putting only as much salt as you need in a clearly-labeled pill bottle rather than bringing a whole kitchen-sized container.

The same thing is true about how much pepper, milk, butter, and cheese you cart with you. You can bring a variety of spices in small bottles zipped in a plastic bag.

Food Safety

Thoroughly wash your hands before and after handling food. Wash dishes and utensils thoroughly before you pack them and then wash all items carefully each time you use them.

Some foods need to be stored on ice or they will go bad. Most food goes bad over time anyhow, and you should check the expiration dates on the packaging. Remember that repackaging food from its original container may hurry this process. Food that smells, looks, or tastes different than it normally does should not be served.

Washing Utensils

Always use a three-stage process of hot wash water containing a little biodegradable soap, hot rinse water, and finally a cold sanitizing rinse water. Dishes should be scraped off before they are put in the hot wash to keep it from silting up. Remember, just because eating utensils and dishes look clean does not mean they are germ free. If you ever have the displeasure of suffering stomach cramps or diarrhea from eating contaminated food,

you'll never let it happen again!

When you are finished cleaning up dishes, don't forget to properly dispose of the dishwater. For a short campout you may simply strain any food residue out of the water, put the waste in the trash, and take the water into the woods and fling the water out over a wide area. For a longer stay, dig a sump hole near camp. This hole should be about two feet deep. Pour strained water into the hole and it will soak into the ground. When you break camp, fill it in and try to leave the area in a natural appearing state. You want to keep such water or food residue away from camp to avoid attracting wildlife looking for a free meal.

FOOD FOR A BASE CAMPSITE

When you don't have to carry it on your back, you can afford to bring some of the comforts of home with you, such as a propane stove top. Since cooking is not as much of a challenge, you get a bit more creative latitude in what you prepare.

You will have more fun if you keep your recipes simple and relatively quick. In fact, you may want to plan something different that you would not try at home, such as cooking an egg in an orange peel cup or baking in a Dutch oven.

The following menu suggestions and recipes are based upon an essay by Brian Boone.

Chili

A big pot of chili is an ideal campsite dinner. Most anything you'd want or need to put in it comes from a can or an envelope and tastes great, and it's so versatile that, beyond the base ingredients, a lot of variations are suitable. One note: Coolers keep food chilled and relatively safe, but not at refrigerator levels. So, if you're going to cook your chili with ground beef or turkey, make it on the first night you're there if you've just got a cooler—you don't want to get sick eating spoiled meat and ruin a trip.

RECIPE After browning meat over a fire or camp stove in a Dutch oven, pour off some of the fat and add two cans of stewed tomatoes, two cans of beans (one each of kidney and pinto), a chopped onion, maybe some jalapeños (if you like spicy food), and a packet of chili powder or chili spice mix. Add about an empty can or two worth of clean water, and let it simmer until everything is soft and warm.

> When you don't have to carry it on your back, you can afford to bring some of the comforts of home with you.

Hot Dogs

Grilling meat is one of the oldest, simplest, and easiest kinds of cookery in the world. There are few things as wonderful as roasting a hot dog on a stick over a roaring campfire, cooking it just enough so that when you bite into it, the skin pops and just a little juice comes out.

Hot dogs have endured as a camping staple because they're inexpensive, come at least eight to a pack and, because they're processed, keep with minimum refrigeration. And while you can grill them on a camp stove, all you really need is a stick and a good fire going.

Pancakes

Pancakes, hotcakes, flapjacks (whatever you want to call them) are an old-fashioned, simple food; something that's easy to make and very filling. They require few ingredients, all of which are easy to pack and store.

RECIPE Here's a simple recipe that dates back to the 1860s: Take three large spoonfuls of flour (white or wheat), add a pinch of salt, and stir in enough water to make a creamy batter. Coat the bottom of a skillet with fat (maybe fat saved from cooking bacon or sausage, as long as it is recent or has been kept in a cooler) and pour in the batter. Flip when the edges curl.

RECIPE Another recipe, from the 20th century: 3 cups flour, a tablespoon of salt, a tablespoon of baking powder, two eggs, two cups of milk—mix the dry and the wet, and then combine.

Cornbread

You could bring a premade cornbread mix, but it's just as easy to make it from scratch in front of the fire. All that's required is cornmeal, salt, water, a little grease, and a skillet.

RECIPE Pour half a cup of cornmeal into a bowl and work in spoonful of fat (bacon grease or butter). Stir in water, and add salt to taste. Coat a skillet with grease, and heat over the fire until it starts to smoke. Pour in the mixture, but leave room on each side so you can flip the bread over, because you'll have to flip it over when the bottom is browned. When it's done, serve warm, and cut into triangular slices like cake or pizza.

Chili Pie

It's a pie in name only, although the end result does mimic a pie, with chips for a crust and chili and other ingredients as the filling. Chili pie, also known as chili cheese pie, is a popular item at food stands and sporting events in the South, but it started off as an easy campfire meal made from mostly nonperishable ingredients.

RECIPE Heat up two cans of chili (or make your own, of course) in a Dutch oven. Line a bowl with corn chips or tortilla chips. Top the chips with the warm chili, diced onions, and shredded cheddar cheese.

Franks and Beans

If camping had an official food, it would be beans. These can be prepared and served any number of ways, but this is a simple method with just a couple of extra ingredients that turns beans—which are filling since they're loaded with both fiber and protein—from a side dish into a meal. **RECIPE** Cut up a package of hot dogs into slices and fry them with some onions in a skillet until the onions brown. Pour off the excess fat. Add a can or two of baked beans, and stir constantly to prevent sticking. Serve it hot—and, if you've got some, with ketchup.

Baked Potatoes

We've covered skillet and pot cooking, open fire cooking, and stick cooking—have you ever cooked anything outdoors in just tin foil? Similar to how potatoes get baked and steamed to fluffy perfection when they're at the bottom of a clambake is the campfire method. First, poke some holes through the potatoes skin with a fork. Wrap the potato in tin foil, making sure to pack it tightly. Place the potato on a hot bed of coals or on a rock next to a low fire. It'll be ready in about half an hour, but check to see if the potato is cooked by poking it once more with a fork.

Broiled Fish

If you're camping near a waterway, you might be lucky or skilled enough to catch yourself a main dinner course. Broiled fish, particularly trout, is a camping must. It's also another way to "rough it" and practice some camping ingenuity by making a rustic broiler (which works for steak as well as fish).

Find a forked branch, hold the fish inside it, and then run two or three sticks in across the width and length of the fish, with the ends resting alternately on the top and bottom of the sides of the branch so as to hold the fish in place. Place the handle of the broiler in the ground so that the "netting" of the broiler and the fish rests over the coals or fire. Broil for about five minutes on each side. (Always check to see if a fishing license is required and if fishing is allowed, in many state and national parks it isn't.)

Hobo Pies and Sandwiches

What's for lunch when camping? For pocket sandwiches filled with hot, juicy fillings, invest $20 in a cooking iron, also known as a hobo pie maker or camping press. It consists of two small, hinged metal plates that fit together at the end of two long handles (for safe handling over a fire).

A hobo pie is a specific foodstuff, and usually a dessert: two slices of bread, butter, and pie filling mashed and heated in the cooking iron until it's an encapsulated, compact treat.

You can make all kinds of hot, simple Panini sandwiches with a cooking iron, particularly grilled cheese or even a Reuben.

Bacon or Sausage

Either bacon or sausage is a great way to ease into cooking outdoors since you basically keep heating it and turning it over until it is done. Prepare the pan with either butter or a non-stick cooking spray like Pam and make sure it is done before you serve it.

Egg Dishes

Eggs are a versatile friend at camp. They can be fried or scrambled, but what's more they can work together with bread to make either one-eyed jacks or French toast. Just be sure you keep the eggs at the right temperature until they are used.

Cold Cereals

For camp breakfasts, cold cereals are instant and almost impossible to overcook. You can make them more healthful by adding fresh fruit, but try the combination at home to make sure you like it.

S'mores

So s'mores aren't technically a meal. But a s'more is a great snack and camping is a vacation, so why not have a graham cracker-marshmallow-chocolate sandwich for dessert?

They're a great camping food because none of the ingredients require refrigeration and anyone who can hold a stick can make one. Here's how you put one together: **RECIPE** Take two marshmallows, poke them on a stick, and toast them on an open flame, turning until the marshmallows are brown. Place them on half a graham cracker and make a sandwich with a square of chocolate on the other cracker half.

FOOD FOR BACKPACKERS

Backpacking food choices center around the all-important need to balance variety and good nutrition with a lightweight pack. The perfect balance point varies among individual hikers but some of the suggestions below work for the great majority of boys.

There are freeze-dried backpacker meals which are very convenient but rather pricey. If you don't want to throw money at the problem or need ultra light rations for hiking the Appalachian Trail, do like generations have before you and make your own chow.

What works for you might be different than what works for other people. Still there are recommended foods that have stood the test of time in the laboratory of the great outdoors. The following is based upon an essay by Claude Freaner of Lake Ridge, Virginia.

Food for New Hikers

Several experienced boys may think of themselves as gourmet cooks on backpack outings. Of course a new boy going on his first hike, probably for the first time in his life, is "leaving civilization and Mom." We would like to suggest food for these inexperienced cooks that usually is nutritious, is always something he will eat, and is easy to fix, particularly when he is tired.

> **Please do not pack more food for a meal than you will eat, because you have to carry it on your back.**

These recommendations are relatively easy to fix and are appealing to most boys. Use your camping equipment and practice cooking some of these meals at home on a weekend. This way, you will already know what you like and how to fix it. Other than freeze-dried eggs, nearly all of the food items listed are available at local supermarkets.

You will notice a distinct lack of vegetables in these meals. If you like vegetables at home and want to take some hiking, then by all means add them to the menus.

Feel free to rearrange these items - these are merely suggestions. As your experience grows, you may like to add in some of the options. Please do not pack more food for a meal than you will eat, because you have to carry it on your back. For example, don't pack a 16 oz.

jar of instant orange drink - put enough for one cup of juice into a baggie and tie with a twister seal. If the item is already in a single serving size, such as individual powdered drink packets or hot cocoa packets, then leave it in its original wrapper.

Put all the ingredients for a single meal into a single larger baggie or sealable plastic bag. Then put all the bags into a small trash bag, or plastic grocery bag, and tie shut. This way, all food is together for a single meal and not lost throughout your backpack.

Breakfast Suggestions

Instant oatmeal, powdered orange drink, hot cocoa, dried fruit. Simple and straightforward and almost impossible to mess up.

Bagel with jelly, powdered orange drink, hot cocoa, dried fruit. Bagels are the preferred bread for hikers. They taste good, don't crush, and won't dry out appreciably.

Bacon (2 slices), freeze-dried scrambled egg, bagel (pre-buttered), dried fruit, hot cocoa. Take two strips of bacon, cut in half, and pre-cook at home until it's almost done (still a bit limp). Wrap in plastic wrap securely. Bacon prepared this way will keep for a few days and can be easily reheated in your frying pan.

MENU Two breakfast bars or Pop-Tarts, powdered orange drink, hot cocoa, dried fruit. Involves very little work and very little cleanup.

MENU Pancakes, bacon, syrup/butter, hot cocoa. Buy the pancake mix that only needs to add water, and put just enough for 2 or 3 pancakes in a baggie. For syrup, get an extra one next time you go to a fast food place in the morning, or you can mix a one-quart package of powdered drink mix with only a little water. For butter, put some margarine into 1 or 2 of the little plastic salsa containers that come with Mexican take-out food.

MENU Dry cereal (pre-sugared variety), powdered milk, hot cocoa, dried fruit.

Lunch Suggestions

The best time to eat lunch when backpacking is from about one hour after breakfast until about one hour before dinner, continuously. In other words, frequent small snacks of complex carbohydrates all day long. That way the body has a constant source of energy available and you are less likely to get too tired. We generally recommend nibbling on trail mix all morning and afternoon, with a little more substantial food for lunch. Carbohydrates come in two main types, simple and complex. Simple carbohydrates are sugars. These cause a rush of energy that lasts an hour or so and leaves you with a jittery feeling from low blood sugar/too much insulin. Your system yo-yos back and forth and you don't really have the sustained energy you need. Complex carbohydrates are like tiny time capsules of energy: the body needs to digest them, and when it does they release energy for a long period with no waste products. Examples are breads, cereals, beans, pasta, etc.

Trail mix is a good snack food for the day-long lunch. You can buy trail mix already put together at most supermarkets. You can also mix your own and put in exactly what you like. Most trail mixes consist of dried fruit, nuts, seeds, etc. A favorite recipe for Adventuring age boys is one part of M&Ms, two parts peanuts, and one part raisins. You can also throw in a little shredded coconut and some dried banana chips. Other good things include shelled sunflower seeds, carob, mixed nuts,

or pretzel sticks. (Go easy on the candy part - it's better to have less candy and more other stuff.) As to how much you will need, for each day of hiking the most you will need is a double handful (less than a cup, if you have to measure it). By comparison, one pound of trail mix will last for a week in the high Sierras. Whatever you get, make sure you like it by trying it at home first.

Bagels are great breads to take along for the more substantial food break around noon. Make some up at home by cutting them in half and putting jelly and/or peanut butter in it, then wrapping it in plastic wrap. Crackers are also good. Granola bars are also a good form of complex carbohydrates.

You should stay away from fats entirely during the day while hiking, as the body takes a fair amount of time to digest fats and convert them to energy. Some fat in the evening meal is good for a hiker, as the body can make use of it while asleep, but it is not good for you while working hard. Jerky, salami sticks, beef

sticks, dry salami, etc. are good meats to take along, but only in small amounts for lunches. Other foods that are good are sardines, ham spread, chicken spread, and so forth, although you will have to carry the weight of the can around with you. In addition, small chunks of cheese or a package of string cheese also taste good. Remember, however, that meats and cheeses contain a lot of fat and you should not have much of this during the day; the best hiking lunch going is a peanut butter and jelly sandwich.

Dinner Suggestions

This is the second most important meal for your physical needs (breakfast is first), but the most important for your mental well-being. By the time dinner rolls around, you will be tired, your feet will hurt, your patience will be thin, and you'll be very hungry. This means the meals need to be simple and quick to fix and appealing to your palate as well as containing the right foods for your body. The evening meal is when you should eat the majority of the day's supply of protein and fats. Since fats take more time to digest than carbohydrates, your body will be using the fats and proteins to repair itself while you're asleep.

The ingredients and possible dinners listed below are always changing but will give you an idea what's available. All it takes is a little imagination. When you must repackage things that need directions, cut out the directions from the box, put into the baggie with the food, and then seal with a twister; rewrite the directions in simple language on a piece of paper, portioned according to the amount you will prepare, and include it with the food.

Try to include soup with each dinner; this is to help get more water back into your system to prevent dehydration, and also gives you something quick to eat while the rest of the meal is cooking. Listed below are some ideas for new hikers. If you really want some more vegetables, bring carrot and celery sticks. Desserts can be just about anything. Instant puddings mixed with dry milk are always good. Other alternatives are commercial fruit pies or bakery items, but the best are homemade cookies or brownies.

MENU **Chicken Noodle powdered soup, hamburger patty, mashed potatoes, corn, punch, fruit pie.** Make up the hamburger patty at home and freeze it. As you get ready to go on Friday afternoon, wrap the frozen patty in foil, shiny side in, and seal in a small sealable plastic bag. Buy instant mashed potatoes and take one serving sealed in a bag. Add a dash of powdered milk to make it creamier. Buy frozen whole-kernel corn; send one serving along, sealed in a bag. Wrap the hamburger and corn in your spare T-shirt for insulation; it will thaw slowly during the day Saturday and be ready to cook at night. For punch, we recommend artificially powdered drink mix as they are light weight and taste good. Fry the hamburger until done enough.

`MENU` **Vegetable powdered soup instant noodles, bagel, small can chicken, punch.** Dump the chicken into the instant noodles while they are cooking.

`MENU` **Chicken noodle powdered soup. small can chicken, 1/2 cup white rice, 1/2 package chicken gravy mix, punch, store-bought dessert snack or bakery item**. Put the rice (regular long-grain rice) in the small pot with 1 cup of water, dump in the chicken, cook for 15 minutes on low heat, covered. Mix the gravy up according to directions, dump in with chicken and rice, re-heat until boiling.

`MENU` **Chicken Broth powdered soup, two hot dogs, 1 tablespoon spaghetti sauce mix, spaghetti noodles, 4 restaurant packets of ketchup, punch, instant pudding with powdered milk.** Break spaghetti noodles into smaller lengths at home. Boil in pot for 10 minutes or so. Pour off most of water, put sauce mix and ketchup into pot with noodles. Cut hot dogs into small chunks and add to noodles and sauce. Cook over low heat, stirring, until hot dogs are hot. Clean out pot after eating out of it, put pre-measured instant pudding and powdered milk into pot, add proper amount of cold water, stir, let stand until thickened, eat.

`MENU` **Chicken Broth powdered soup, 1/2 package macaroni & cheese, small can tuna, corn, punch, homemade chocolate chip cookies.** Repackage the 1/2 of macaroni in a sealable plastic baggie. Also 1/2 of cheese packet in another Ziploc bag, along with some powdered milk. Cook according to directions; add the tuna at the end, reheat, eat.

`MENU` **Chicken Noodle powdered soup, stew, bagel, punch.** Freeze some stew at home in a small 2 by 3 by 4 in Tupperware. Put into a sealable plastic baggie in case of leaks. Put a piece of cake into another sealable container for dessert.

Gourmet Suggestions

Below are listed some ideas for more sophisticated menus that have been field tested.

- Fettuccini Alfredo with White Clam Sauce and fresh Broccoli with Hollandaise Sauce
- Mexican Tacos with Spanish Rice and Refried Beans
- Corned beef, cabbage, and new potatoes (St. Patrick's day)
- Beef Stroganoff with Green Beans and Corn Bread
- Roast Beef, Mashed Potatoes, Peas, Gravy
- Roast Turkey, Mashed Potatoes, Stuffing, Broccoli with Hollandaise Sauce
- Beef Burgundy, Braised Noodles, Steamed Carrots

In Summary

What makes the ideal campsite meal varies from what goes for the ideal backpack meal. If you are carting supplies a few yards from the van to your dining fly, you may want to enjoy a lot of amenities. When everything you eat and everything you use to prepare it must be carried on your back, you'll develop a more sophisticated idea of what it means to "live simply and well." That is a lesson that has many more uses in life than eating on the trail.

Oh, and be sure to remember that this food, just like the glories of nature around you, was provided by our gracious Heavenly Father. Always be in the habit of giving thanks to God before you "dig in".

CHAPTER
12

ROPEWORK

Rope, properly used, is like many other things. Just like a box of nails, a pot of glue, a roll of tape, it can hold things together.

Unlike those other things, rope can be taken off and reused many times! Rope is not merely a tool of sailors and campers. It is used in everything from hanging up a tire swing to rescuing stranded climbers. It is very versatile, and the better you learn to control it, the more indispensable it will become.

You exercise control over rope by learning knots and lashings.

Combine rope with wooden poles and you unleash the ability to build everything from camp gadgets to towers, bridges, gateways, and rafts. The only limits are your imagination and, of course, common sense. Before you start stringing poles, learn how to brace structures, and which lashings work best for each job.

Standing End or Body

Running End

IMPORTANT TERMS

First a few terms, for it is important you know what things are called in order to follow the instructions. Always use the correct terms when teaching these skills to others.

The **standing part** of a rope is everything that's not at either end. Each end is referred to as a **free end**. Some people call the free end that you're using to tie the knot the **running end.**

Sometimes you hear people talk about **making and breaking knots**. That's a fancy way of saying tying and untying knots

If you bend the running end of the rope around to form a hook or U-shape, that hook is a **bight**. If the running end crosses over the top of the standing part of the rope to form an O-shape, it's called an **overhand loop**. If the running end passes under the standing part it is an **underhand loop**.

A **hitch** is a knot that ties a rope to a stationary object. If you tie a knot around a tree or a post, that's a hitch. Just think about cowboys tying their horses to a hitching post.

Bight

Overhand loop

Underhand loop

ALL KNOTS ARE NOT CREATED EQUAL

Every knot has its strengths and weaknesses. That's why you want to pick the right kind of knot for the job and tie it (make it) the right way. Being sure the knot slides into position correctly is called **dressing** the knot.

You'll learn some basic knots in this chapter that will cover most situations, and all of them have three things in common—they are easy to make, they stay made as long as you need them, and they are easy to break.

TYING KNOTS

TWO HALF HITCHES

Two half hitches form a loop around an object that can be easily adjusted, much the way you adjust your belt.

As you read this text and compare it to the photographs, it will help you practice your knot-tying terms. You want to know these terms quite well so you can teach others.

First you pass the **running end** of the rope around the post. For a moment, it's a **bight**. You take the running end and cross it under the **standing part** and now it's an **underhand loop**.

Now bring the running end over the standing part, coming up through the underhand loop, turning it into a **half hitch**. Then take the running end around the standing part once more and tie another half hitch. You pull it snugly against the pole, which is how you **dress** the knot.

Two Half Hitches form a knot that can easily be adjusted.

TAUT-LINE HITCH

The taut-line hitch is used for guy lines on a tent or dining fly, or anywhere else you need a rope to stay tight—or taut—by adjusting it as needed.

Pass the running end of the rope around a tent stake. Bring that end over and under the standing part of the line to form a loop, then twice through the loop. Now go a bit further up the standing part and bring the running end over, under, and through a loop. Now dress the knot by working any slack out of it and you slide the hitch to adjust the tension.

BOWLINE

Now for a knot that can't be adjusted, and for a very good reason. Sometimes you need a loop that cannot slip, especially when you're trying to pull someone out of danger. There are other uses for this knot too, especially in attaching guy lines to a tent or dining fly.

If you and a friend tie a bowline around yourselves and then lean back, you'll be impressed with the strength and comfort of this knot.

Make a small overhand loop in the standing part of your rope. Pass the running end up through the loop, around behind the standing part, then back down into the loop. Make the knot by pulling the standing part of the rope away from the loop. A good way to remember this is to think of the running end as a rabbit who pops out of the rabbit hole, runs around behind the tree, then jumps back down the hole.

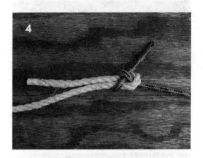

SHEET BEND

The sheet bend is a lot like a bowline, but it is used to tie two different ropes together. Think of it like plugging in an extension cord. What makes this a great knot is that two ropes of different thickness can be securely fastened together, something that's hard to do with most other knots.

Put a bend in the running end of the thicker rope and hold it in one hand. Pass the running end of the smaller rope through the bend, then take it around behind the bend,

then on across the front of the bend and tuck it under its own standing part. Make the knot by pulling the standing part of the smaller rope.

The Taut-Line Hitch
will stay tight, but you can adjust it.
The Bowline
is a loop that will not slip.
The Sheet Bend
allows you to tie two ropes of different thickenesses

SQUARE KNOT

The square knot is simple to tie if you just remember the phrase "right over left, left over right." Take the two ends you plan to join, and pass the right end over the left rope. Now that the ropes have changed hands, pass the left end over the right end. Now make the knot by pulling it together.

TIMBER HITCH

While the timber hitch was originally designed for dragging logs with a rope, it will be very useful for you when you take on lashings.

Pass the free end of the rope around the log. Now loop it around the standing part and twist the rope around itself three or more times. Pull the rope to tighten the hitch against the log. This knot will break easily when tension is released.

Square Knot

CLOVE HITCH

The clove hitch is very useful for tying your horse to the hitching post or for starting and ending most lashings. It can also be used to close the neck of a sack of potatoes or pretty much anything else you need to bag securely.

Bring the running end over and under a pole, then bring it around a second time, crossing over the first wrap to make an X shape. When you bring the running end around a third time, tuck it under the X. Now pull the running end to make the knot.

BUILDING THINGS

LASHINGS

Now you want to build things ranging from useful gadgets to exciting
structures using wooden poles and
rope. To do this easily and safely
you need to know your lashings. A
lashing is more involved than just
tying a knot. It is a special way
of winding ropes to attach poles
(called **spars**) together tightly.

As with knots, there is a language associated with lashings.
Learn these terms as you study
lashings and use them properly when you teach others.

A **wrap** is a turn made around
two spars to hold the spars
together. Wraps are made tightly
in tightly packed groups, three for
a simple lashing like the square
lashing, more for other lashings
that have to hold tight at an angle.

A **frap** is a couple of turns
of the rope between the spars
to pull the wraps tighter.

SQUARE LASHINGS

A square lashing can be used for a
flagpole. It connects two poles that
cross at a right angle. Tie a clove
hitch in the bottom close to the
junction of the poles. Make three
tight wraps around both poles. Make
two tight fraps around the wraps
between the poles, pulling the rope
tightly, then finish the lashing with
a clove hitch on the top pole. It can
help you pull fraps tight if you use
a small stick to wind some rope
around and use it as a handle.

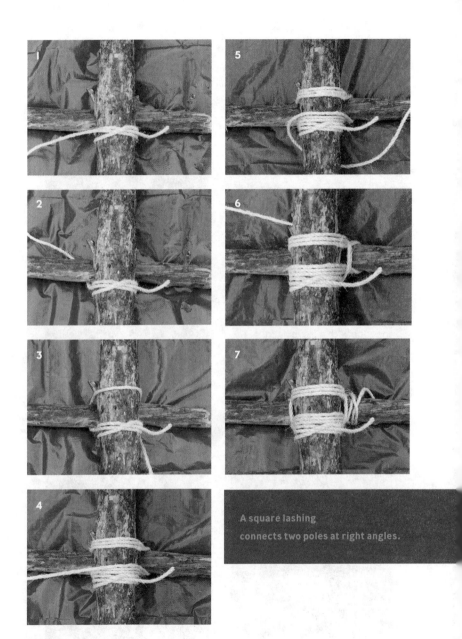

A square lashing
connects two poles at right angles.

Square Lashings

DIAGONAL LASHINGS

The diagonal lashing firmly binds poles together that do not cross at a right angle.

Tie a timber hitch diagonally around both poles and tighten it. Now make three wraps diagonally around the poles crossing the timber hitch.

Make three more wraps around the poles in the opposite angle. Tighten it with two fraps between the poles and tie off the rope with a clove hitch.

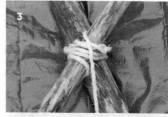

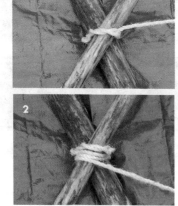

SHEAR LASHINGS

The shear lashing acts as a hinge allowing the poles to be moved into their final position. Place the poles to be joined side by side and tie a clove hitch to one of them. Then make three loose wraps around the poles. Put two loose fraps around the wraps between the poles. Finish it off with a clove hitch around the other pole. You can now turn the poles around this lashing to form an angle. To make the shear lashing more secure, you can use racked wrapping instead of plain wrapping. With racked wrapping, weave the rope between the poles, and then frap.

TRIPOD LASHINGS

The tripod lashing is a close relative of the shear lashing and can be used to suspend a pot over a fire.

Place the three poles to be bound together parallel to each other. Tie a clove hitch around one of the outside poles. Loosely wrap the rope around the poles at least three times, keeping the turns neatly arranged.

Make two loose fraps on either side of the center pole. Finish it off with a clove hitch on the outside pole opposite of the starting clove hitch. Now you can spread the legs to form a tripod.

If you find your tripod lashing is too loose, here are two options you can try. Substitute racked wrapping for plain wrapping by weaving the wrappings between the poles. You can also start the lashing by laying your poles parallel to each other, with the top of the center pole pointing in the opposite direction of the outside poles. When you spread the legs to form a tripod, this center pole will flip and put a half twist in the lashing.

The tripod lashing can be used to suspend a pot over a fire.

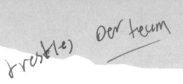

X Trestle

A Trestle

H Trestle

TRESTLES

Trestles are not a type of lashing, but rather a form of bracing you get when you incorporate triangles into your design. The three basic types are the X-trestle, A-tresle, and H-trestle. These add strength to your pioneering project, which can be helpful especially when you plan to rest your weight on it.

The round lashing is very good for making a flagpole.

ROUND LASHINGS

Round lashings bind two poles side by side to form an extension. This is also very good for making a flagpole but should not be used for stringers in weight bearing applications.

Put the two poles side by side where there is a significant amount of overlap of the two ends, otherwise it will not be a stable joining. Tie the poles together with a clove hitch, then make eight very tight wraps around the poles. Use a stick to help you pull the wraps tight. Finish the lashing with a second clove hitch around both poles. You will need to tie two round lashings, one close to the end of each pole, to achieve sturdiness.

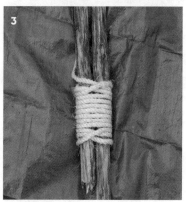

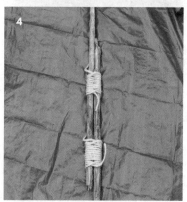

FLOOR LASHINGS

This helpful lashing creates a flat surface for anything from a bridge walkway to a camp table. Now for a new vocabulary word: **stringers**. The stringers are the horizontal poles to which all the **treads** will be attached. The term treads seems to indicate a walking surface such as a bridge, catwalk or raft, but it also applies to poles used to make a roof or a table top.

Place the treads side by side on top of the stringers. Tie a clove hitch around one of the stringers. Now bringing the standing part up and over the first tread you cross over it diagonally and go under the opposite side of the stringer. Done right you will have a series of diagonal "stitches" connecting the treads to the stringer. Finish off that side with a clove hitch around the end of the stringer. Now go down the other stringer attaching the treads from the other side.

Ropework photos: Nyk + Cali Photography (pages 156-161) and Troop FL-714 (pages 163-170)

When you reach

the **end of your rope**,

tie a knot in it

and **hang on**.

—*Thomas Jefferson*

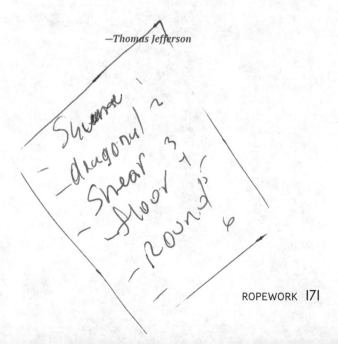

ACADEMICS

13

SCIENCE

Mankind has always been curious, eager to learn new facts and to explore how things work. Science is a way of building our knowledge in a carefully disciplined way using the scientific method.

THE SCIENTIFIC METHOD

It is easy to jump to the wrong conclusion. Let's say you have a cuckoo clock that you believe chimes every hour on the hour.

Then one day the cat jumps up on the desk and swats at the swinging pendulum and the clock stops. Several minutes later you notice it and give the pendulum a little push. It's ticking again, but it no longer chimes on the hour. There went your theory!

The scientific method is designed to prevent you from jumping to the wrong conclusions.

First, ask a question:

This part is harder than it sounds. Many questions have

already been asked by someone else. Maybe your question is, "What makes the cuckoo clock chime?"

Research and form a hypothesis:

Once you have a question, try to learn everything already known about clocks and, based on your findings, you might state, "I think the minute hand is somehow connected to the chime." You want to state your hypothesis in a way that

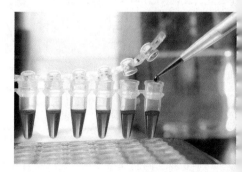

can be easily measured, so you decide to state, "When the minute hand reaches twelve, it somehow signals the clock to chime."

Testing:

You design a test to see if such a signal exists. It involves watching the works while your assistant advances the minute hand. Right at twelve a spike on a gear attached to the minute hand flips a lever on the chime.

Analysis:

You look over your observations and see what conclusions you can draw. You determine that the gears in the clock form a relationship among the moving parts. One result is the starting of the chimes when the minute hand is lined up with the twelve. And your hypothesis is true!

That's a simple way to show the scientific method.

STRENGTHS OF THE SCIENTIFIC METHOD

The scientific method allows you to build up a body of proven knowledge which can be relied upon. If you are trying to study the structure of ice, you no longer have to go back and prove that water is made up of hydrogen and oxygen. While many ideas in science will remain a theory for the foreseeable future, the number of established facts continues to grow each year, each one helping us see nature in clearer focus and giving us a better platform to launch new theories.

The scientific method helps us avoid logical errors. Simple observation may suggest that laying in a hospital bed makes you sick and wearing large shoes gives you big feet! But the scientific method tests these guesses, or hypotheses.

One ancient theory suggested that everything was made of four types of atoms: earth, air, fire, and water. According to that idea, atoms of water were round like ball bearings, so they slipped against each other easily. On the other hand, atoms of earth were shaped like dice and tended to form rough, firm layers like soil and rock. Fire, of course, had sharp points which caused it to be painful and erode wood into a few white ashes.

While it may have appealed to the common sense of our ancestors, such a thing could never pass the test of our modern scientific method.

Some of today's theories may sound every bit as far-fetched, and they should remain theories if they cannot be proven true. The scientific method sets a very high standard of proof.

Oddly enough, some old theories we once thought would never be proven are now accepted fact. We have images of individual atoms that were once thought forever invisible, and weather patterns of prehistoric times have been revealed through the study of Antarctic ice and sea sediments.

Who knows what will be added to the sum of our knowledge during your lifetime? And what theories will come from this proven knowledge? Perhaps you will make a contribution of your own!

FIELDS OF SCIENCE

There are many specialized fields of science. Here are the major categories of scientific pursuit that help us understand our universe.

Geology

Geology studies things that make up the earth and how they are put together. Geologists help find deposits of oil and natural gas. They do things like identify rock

LIMITS OF THE SCIENTIFIC METHOD

The scientific method can only investigate something that can be observed and tested.

It can't prove something doesn't exist, and it can only prove something does exist if it can be directly or indirectly detected.

It can only judge the performance of things that can be reduced to numbers such as the germ killing power of a new drug. It cannot make moral judgments or separate beauty from ugliness.

It cannot tell why things happen, only how they happen. That's why behaviorists speak of your cat "bonding" with you rather than "loving" you, and do not deal with whether or not nature was created to serve a higher purpose. This does not mean that scientists themselves are unfeeling people without opinions about things they can't see or touch, it just means they are limited because some things are harder to prove than others.

samples and try to predict earthquakes and volcanic eruptions. They also study evidence of past life.

Physics

Physics looks at properties of matter, energy and how they behave in time and space. For example, physicists watch the way exotic particles are formed when plasma energy collides with a target. They figure how much fuel it would take to get a satellite into orbit around the moon.

Chemistry

Chemistry examines what makes up matter and how it behaves. A chemist might make many of the new products you hear about such as high impact plastic and food preservatives. They can identify unknown substances in laboratories and help identify health hazards in the environment.

Biology

Biology studies living things and how life works. Biologists do things like discover new species in the rain forest and learn how the brain processes what your eyes see. Some specialize in understanding how the traits that make you unique are stored in your genes.

Ecology

Ecologists chart relationships that living things have with each other and with their non-living environment. To an ecologist, an animal or a plant may be a piece in a bigger puzzle, taking some things from their home and giving other things back. Through their studies they may see what harm the disappearance of a species does to the whole ecosystem.

Astronomy

Astronomy studies heavenly bodies and space. By looking at the pattern of light from stars, astronomers can measure the chemistry of bodies they will never get to visit in person.

They do things like observe feedback from the Mars Landers and help warn us of near-Earth objects.

Meteorology

Meteorology looks at the ever-changing atmosphere. Meteorologists predict weather and study hurricanes and tornadoes. Their work saves money, time, and human lives. They can even play a part in history, like when they were instrumental in setting the best time for the allied invasion of Europe in World War II.

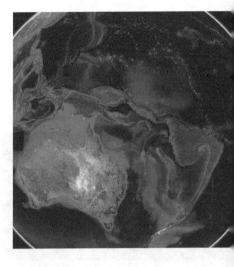

Oceanography

Oceanography studies the restless oceans, which cover 71 percent of our planet. Oceanographers map the ocean floor using sound waves. With 95 percent of the sea still unexplored they will not run out of new frontiers in your lifetime. Some focus on charting the currents of the deep and discovering strange new creatures.

FAITH AND SCIENCE

Faith and Science are two ways of looking at the same reality. God cannot be explained by using the scientific method, but neither can your choice of favorite color. It has been aptly said that science tells us *how* and religion tells us *why*.

As Pope John Paul II stated in *Fides et Ratio*, "Faith and reason are like two wings on which the human spirit rises to the contemplation of truth; and God has placed in the human heart a desire to know the truth—in a word, to know himself—so that, by knowing and loving God, men and women may also come to the fullness of truth about themselves."

The fields of science, in order to flourish in true objectivity, need people like you who do not reject the idea of a God as blind superstition.

There are some people who have faith that there is no God. While the word "faith" looks odd associated with the idea of atheism, the scientific method has no means of proving that someone does not exist. That makes atheism a belief that falls short of the threshold of the scientific method that is so essential to proof.

Some people say that science provides other explanations for natural phenomena that make the existence of God unnecessary. When you really think about it, that is a foolish argument. Let's say there are muddy dog prints on your kitchen floor and you own a dog with feet that size that likes to track in mud. If someone argued that another dog with muddy feet could have been sneaked into the house to make the prints before being carried away unseen that would give another possible explanation. But would it make the idea that your own dog did it "unnecessary"? Would it reduce your idea to mere superstition?

Ask the people who study science for a living. The Pew Research Center took a poll in 2009 that showed a majority of scientists believe in God or some form of higher power. The complex inter-relationships among living things in an ecosystem, and the careful conditions that had to be met for life to exist on Earth suggest some form of intelligent design to many of the world's most educated people. One of them was the late Dr. Louis S. B. Leakey who discovered many fossils of early men. He firmly believed in God.

The fields of science, in order to flourish in true objectivity, need people like you who do not reject the idea of a God as blind superstition. Only when all options are on the table, including the idea that our universe exists for a reason, can the scientific method truly escape from observer bias and operate as intended.

SCIENCE AND ETHICS

There are questions that need to be settled for any prospective scientist, like, "How far we should go in pursuit of knowledge?" and, "What uses of that knowledge are right in God's eyes?" As we see controversy over genetically modified plants in agriculture, questions about when life begins, debates about the use of human embryos for stem cell research, and misgivings about the use of nuclear

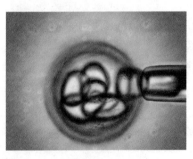

power and nuclear weapons, we realize that every advance of science brings its own moral dilemmas and burden of responsibility. Our appropriate pursuit of knowledge and righteous use of it are a measure of our human character.

Fortunately, there is a growing body of scientists that elects to work under strong ethical standards both in how they increase our knowledge and in how that knowledge is used.

THE FINAL ANALYSIS

It is not so much our level of knowledge as our thirst to know that points out the image of God within us. God could have given us answers—instead, He gave us curiosity and a world of wonders. What a blessing to take it all in!

No amount of experimentation can ever **prove me right**; a single experiment can **prove me wrong**.

—*Albert Einstein*

CHAPTER

14

TECHNOLOGY

Technology is the use of knowledge to solve practical problems. Since it is built upon knowledge, great advances in technology usually follow great advances in science. You can tell how important it is when you see history divided into periods dominated by technological skills. We are used to speaking of a Stone Age, Bronze Age, atomic age, space age, and an information age.

THE POWER OF KNOWLEDGE

We tend to associate the word technology with "high tech," yet some of the most important discoveries and inventions of man—fire and the wheel—are among the simplest. A technology as basic as washing hands to kill germs saves thousands of lives each year.

Many of the things we enjoy are the result of discoveries throughout time. When you camp, the tent you sleep in combines ancient technologies of shelter and rope-making, nineteenth-century weaving, twentieth-century synthetic materials and twenty-first century breathable construction. Even the

fan in your computer case came from the Ancient Greek "Archimedes screw." The electricity that turns the fan was the same mysterious force those Greeks called "elektron."

> Some of the most important discoveries and inventions of man—fire and the wheel—are among the simplest.

It is precisely our habit of adding on new levels of sophistication that drives our civilization forward one generation at a time. No matter when you live, it seems that your technology will be more advanced than your parents' tools and not quite as advanced as your children's gadgets! This can be good and bad.

THE PROMISE AND THE PERIL

The desire to make knowledge useful is powerful. If you discovered a way to turn yourself invisible, it would start out as a great scientific break-through.

Within moments of your discovery, you would make it a technology as your mind raced with all the exciting possibilities. Some of them would be good things like solving crimes or viewing timid wildlife up close. Others of them would be harmless like pulling pranks on your friends. Then would come bigger and bigger temptations. What if you could convince your unpopular neighbors that their house was haunted? What if you could walk into a bank vault and stuff your pockets with bills? What if you invaded countries with invisible armies and left their rulers cowering in the dust at your feet?

Applied scientific knowledge is a powerful force. But it also comes with great responsibility.

For every nuclear reactor to light your house there is a nuclear weapon to destroy it. For every camera to take pictures of your family vacation, there is another camera that records inappropriate images. With the invention of the telephone came abusive phone calls.

As responsible Trailmen, we must ensure that technology walks hand-in-hand with righteous responsibility to keep its promise of a better life for all.

FASTER AND HIGHER

It may be hard to imagine that people once played chess by mail. Now friends play together in 3-D worlds in real time. Rather than waiting a week for your letter to cross America and a week for the reply to come back, you pick up the phone, write an e-mail, tweet, IM, or have a videoconference.

Imagine what it was like voting for President of the United States in the days before the telegraph. Poll results were delivered by horsemen. Now we watch election returns on live TV and know the outcome before midnight on election day.

In the 1840's when many people wanted to settle out west, they would take an uncomfortable and dangerous five-month wagon ride across America. Now a non-stop jet flight from New York City to San Diego takes just under six hours.

The rapid speed of communication and transportation has greatly affected how we live and work. It has helped us form communities spanning thousands of miles while at the same time making us less familiar with the people in our own neighborhood. We tend to be more united by interests than by geography. Unfortunately it tempts us to fill our social needs without getting out into the real world and making friends we can touch. It may isolate us from nature.

ISOLATION FROM NATURE

Long ago, houses tended to be very small. They gave people shelter at night, during inclement weather, and at mealtimes. Most of the day was spent outdoors in the sunshine and fresh air.

Climate control gave people welcome relief from summer heat and winter chill. Unfortunately,

it also had the effect of driving people indoors away from the weather to a climate of their own choosing. The informal contact people had with their neighbors died off with the front porch swing as windows and doors were sealed tight against the elements. That, coupled with long commutes in air-conditioned cars, reduces still further our contact with neighbors as we shop, work, and attend church. It reduces the amount of healthy exercise we receive and tempts us to rely on supplements to bolster our unwholesome diets.

Your experiences as a member of a Troop become even more important as a way of keeping in contact with God's nature and good friends.

TYPES OF TECHNOLOGY

Unlike science, technology is not easily broken into a few major fields. However some of the ways technology serves us today are listed here.

Transportation

A global network of highways, railroads, air routes, and seaways keep people and goods in motion around our nation and our world.

Easy access to quick transportation has changed the way people build cities and neighborhoods. Medieval people lived in town next to their place of business or on the farm. Now it is not uncommon for people to live a half-hour's drive or more away from work so they can take advantage of living in rural counties while working in large cities.

Information

No longer restricted to wires, our sounds, images, and documents race at the speed of light, using satellites in earth orbit. The dividing line between telephones and computers is getting more blurry each year. Cell phones allow you to surf the internet. People are used to—and sometimes dependent upon—immediate answers to their questions.

Aerospace

When Neil Armstrong stepped onto the lunar surface, mankind inhab-

ited more than one heavenly body. Now remotely-controlled rovers travel the surface of Mars, partly to gather research for the first human visitor. You will live to see it, and you may even be that visitor!

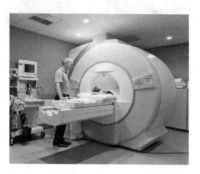

Healthcare

Advances in healthcare have increased the average lifespan of people and helped patients cope better with loss of vision, missing limbs, and lack of mobility. Cancer is no longer the death sentence it used to be. More and more diseases and conditions are yielding to the advance of medical technology.

Food and Agriculture

The challenges of supplying the American armed forces during World Wars I and II changed the way crops were grown and pushed for the development of additives to preserve food and lock in flavor

and aroma during storage. Packing technology, coupled with advances in transportation, keep our favorite foods on the menu year round. We also enjoy exotic foods from distant lands at an affordable price.

Textiles

We think about modern breathable fabrics as technology's contribution to clothing. Yet power looms and machine-patterned cloth were not always around. When cloth was made by hand looms, checks and patterns had to be painstakingly created.

Industrial

Machines that create the goods and services we need have become more and more sophisticated. Industrial robots do repetitive work without suffering from boredom, illness, or injury.

Military

Every war since the American Revolution has seen major advances in military technology. During the Civil War, balloons were used for aerial reconnaissance, and orders were transmitted by telegraph. Today, there are nuclear missiles that could achieve in moments a greater destructive force than all our previous wars put together.

Truly, technology has impacted every area of our lives, and it takes men of great character to make sure technology makes the world a better place and improves the lives of all people as it advances.

ADVANCEMENT

CHAPTER

15

EARNING
NAVIGATOR RANKS

Your first achievements as a Navigator Trailman will be earning the skill ranks of Recruit Trailman, Able Trailman, and Ready Trailman. These ranks recognize your growing ability to get along safely and comfortably in the outdoors and to be a contributor in making your fellow Trailmen, your Troop, and its activities a success.

RECRUIT RANK

This is the joining rank that concentrates on being safe and learning how to plug in to all the resources available to you in your Troop. You will attend your first hikes and campouts, and make new friends in your Troop.

ABLE TRAILMAN RANK

This rank concentrates on being comfortable in the outdoors and building on your knowledge and understanding of outdoor skills. You will learn about camping, nature, service, and working together in a patrol.

READY TRAILMAN RANK

This rank concentrates on making you a useful Trailman to have around camp – a Ready Trailman is skilled in the outdoors. You'll continue to learn about outdoor skills and service, and also focus on leadership and faith. A successful Trailman is expected to have a positive, can-do attitude about most things in life. Working diligently as a Ready Trailman will help you develop that attitude.

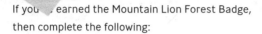

JIT TRAILMAN

If you 〔 . 〕earned the Mountain Lion Forest Badge,
then complete the following:

Traditions:

_____✓_____ Agree to live by the Trailman Oath.

_____✓_____ Give your Patrol Leader's name, patrol name, and patrol yell.

✗

Leader Conference:

_____✓_____ Discuss Troop safety.

_____✓_____ Discuss advancement program.

If you are a new member of the Trail Life USA program, complete the following:

Traditions:

_____✓_____ Memorize and agree to live by the Trailman Oath.

_____✓_____ Memorize the Trailman Motto.

_____✓_____ Demonstrate the Trailman sign and describe when to use it.

_____✓_____ Demonstrate the Trailman salute and describe when to use it.

_____✓_____ Demonstrate the Trailman handshake.

_____ Give your Patrol Leader's name, patrol name, and patrol yell.

Citizenship:

_____✓____ Memorize the Pledge of Allegiance.

_____✓_____ Demonstrate properly folding the American flag.

Leader Conference:

_____✓_____ Discuss Troop safety.

_____✓_____ Discuss advancement program.

_____   _____

Trailmaster   Date

ABLE TRAILMAN

Prerequisite: Earn the Recruit Trailman Rank.

Trail Badge Work:

_____ Complete any four of the nine Trail Badges required for the Ready Trailman Rank (Aquatics, Camping, Fire Ranger, First Aid, Our Flag, Outdoor Cooking, Ropework, Trail Skills, and Woods Tools).

_____ Earn an additional three Trail Badges of your choice. (Note: The Horizon Required Trail Badges cannot be earned in the Navigators program)

Servant Service:

_____ Complete 15 hours of service for each year since joining Navigators. Record your hours on the service chart in your handbook and have them verified by an adult.

Troop Involvement:

_____ Maintain a level of Troop meeting attendance acceptable to your Trailmaster (typically 60% or better).

_____ Participate in at least 8 Troop activities since becoming a Navigator, not including regular meetings. Record each activity on the activity chart in your handbook (Trips, camp, community outings, etc.) and have each one verified by an adult.

Mark Your Progress:

_____ Successfully complete an Advancement Conference with your Trailmaster or Trail Guide.

_____ Successfully complete a Board of Review.

_____   _____
Board of Review Chair   Date

READY TRAILMAN

Prerequisite: Earn the Able Trailman Rank.

Trail Badge Work:

_____ Complete the following nine required Trail Badges: Aquatics, Camping, Fire Ranger, First Aid, Our Flag, Outdoor Cooking, Ropework, Trail Skills, and Woods Tools.

_____ Earn a total of five elective Trail Badges of your choice since joining as a Navigator. (Note: The Horizon Required Trail Badges cannot be earned in the Navigators program)

Servant Service:

_____ Complete 15 hours of service for each year as a Navigator. Record your hours on the service chart in your handbook and have them verified by an adult.

Troop Involvement:

_____ Maintain a level of Troop meeting attendance acceptable to your Trailmaster (typically 60% or better).

_____ Participate in at least 16 Troop activities since becoming a Navigator, not including regular meetings. Record each activity on the activity chart in your handbook (trips, camp, community outings, etc.) and have each one verified by an adult.

Leadership:

Since earning the Able Trailman Rank, complete one of the following leadership options:

_____ Serve as a Junior Patrol Leader for a minimum of six months.

_____ At five troop meetings, demonstrate your leadership ability by planning and instructing Recruit or Able Trailmen in significant Ready Trailmen required Trail Badge skills approved by your Trailmaster or Trail Guide.

_____ At five troop meetings, demonstrate your leadership ability by planning and instructing a Woodlands Trail group in significant skills approved by your Trailmaster or Trail Guide and the Woodlands Trail Ranger.

Faith:

Complete one of the following Faith Building Activity Options and discuss it with your Trailmaster or Trail Guide:

_____ Any Trail Life USA Values Branch Trail Badge

_____ The Navigators Christian Faith Activities Option

_____ A Navigators level Christian Religious Recognition (according to your denomination)

_____ A Navigators Trail Life USA approved father-and-son Group Discipleship Program, such as The Manhood Journey Program

Mark Your Progress:

_____ Successfully complete an Advancement Conference with your Trailmaster or Trail Guide.

_____ Successfully complete a Board of Review.

_____   _____

Board of Review Chair   Date

ABLE TRAILMAN RANK SERVICE HOURS

Service Type	Date	Hours	Verified by

ABLE TRAILMAN RANK ACTIVITIES

Service Type	Date from	Date to	Nights	Verified by	
Hit the trail / Chivo trail	9/10/2017	9/10/2017	N/A	Adrian Floores	trail Guide.
Chumash trail Hike	1/13/2018		1	Adrian Flory	
Warrior games	2/16/2018	2/18/18	2	A Flores	
Hike - White face	8/26/17	8/26/17	0	A Flory	
VSS IOWA	11/17/18	11/14/18	1	A Flores	

READY TRAILMAN RANK SERVICE HOURS

Service Type	Date	Hours	Verified by

READY TRAILMAN RANK ACTIVITIES

Service Type	Date from	Date to	Nights	Verified by

GOALS / NOTES

EARNING
ADVENTURER AWARDS

If you were involved in middle school, you've probably earned the rank of Ready Trailman and shown yourself to be an all-around Trailman. Now you are ready to grow beyond the basics and tap into your wellspring of potential. You will do this as a member of an Adventurers Unit. Adventurers is an advanced program that sets you apart as an older, more skilled member of the Troop. The program offers you more freedom to set and achieve your own goals, and to chart your own adventures.

Adventurers Trailmen do not need to earn additional skill *ranks* because they have already demonstrated their ability as a Trailman. Now they earn *awards* for personal growth. The trail to the peak pauses briefly at the *Journey Award* and the *Horizon Award*, and leads to the highest achievement you can reach in Trail Life USA—the *Freedom Award*. The Freedom award will follow you through life as a badge of honor.

THE ADVENTURERS EXPERIENCE

Your Adventurers Unit is headed up by an adult called the Advisor, assisted by one or more Trail Guides. Youth leaders occupy the offices of First Officer, Second Officer, Quartermaster, and Patrol Leader. You will have unprecedented control over the experience, and what you learn by participating in planning and carrying out your program will benefit you as you enter the job world. You will learn things about yourself as a leader that you might not have the chance to learn in many other settings.

YOUR RELATIONSHIP TO NAVIGATORS

As the most experienced youth in the Troop, the guidance and example of dedicated Adventurers is vital to the development of younger boys. Adults can be great role models, but you are the immediate model the younger Trailmen are following. You are not just working on your own advancement; you are indirectly working on theirs. Do the best job you can.

You will have a pivotal role in setting the monthly program of activities for the Troop. When things come together and everyone has a good time and learns something, you'll feel great. It's a first-rate feeling of accomplishment you get from doing worthwhile things.

The trail to the peak pauses briefly at the *Journey Award* and the *Horizon Award*, and leads to the highest achievement you can reach in Trail Life USA—the *Freedom Award*.

THE JOURNEY AWARD

This is the joining award for the Adventurers Program. It is awarded to Navigators that bridge over to the Adventurers program or boys who join in high school. This is the beginning of the transition period to manhood, active citizenry, and mastering leadership.

THE HORIZON AWARD

The Horizon Trailman completes the required body of knowledge encompassed in the Trail Badge program as his focus changes from knowledge to higher level understanding and gaining wisdom, while reaching new horizons of adventure and personal growth.

THE FREEDOM AWARD

The Freedom Award is the highest recognition on the Adventurers Trail. The program focus moves to Christian manhood with faith building activities, freedom experiences, and the servant leadership project. It is our hope that Trailmen will grow in their Christian walk to experience eternal freedom in Jesus Christ along their Trail to the Freedom Award.

When you earn the award, you become a Freedom Rangeman, who understands that God's plan for us includes certain freedom, but also entails great responsibility.

THE BOY YOU ARE

Sometimes you see the exciting things that adults do and the wonderful places they go and you feel impatient waiting to grow up.

In that process of growing up, it is as if you relive the act of Creation by your birth into a bright, noisy world of chaos. Even as God brought order through Creation, God and those who do His Will bring order into your life through their instruction, example, and care. Getting there is a wondrous process, and you should be glad you have been through it and you should enjoy every day.

Manhood is not something you will experience when you wake on the morning of your 18th birthday. In fact, manhood is something you gradually achieve by degrees in different areas of your life such as your leadership skills, your wisdom, your emotional maturity, and your understanding of freedom as combinations of rights and responsibilities.

Each of these areas of your life will mature at different rates, and at each phase you'll grow to meet the increasingly greater challenges.

THE MAN YOU WILL BE

Because no two men are exactly alike, we cannot give you a check-list of things that make you a man. However, faithful Christians know there are certain things a man is, and certain things he isn't.

A real man *is* someone who accepts responsibility for his own actions, who understands that the world does not owe him a living, and who considers citizenship an obligation as well as a privilege. He understands that manhood emerges, it does not suddenly appear. Fact is, if you live as you should, you will continue to mature throughout your whole earthly life.

A man *is not* someone who turns against the morals and good habits of his youth. Whatever society tells you, getting drunk, committing fornication, abusing drugs, smoking, and drinking are not "rites of passage" that bring you from childhood to manhood. Many fine people who became real men did not feel the need to do these things to achieve maturity.

There is a world of difference between being a grown male and being a real man. A grown male can add a baby to the world, but a real man becomes a father. A grown male may hold a job, but a real man has a career. A grown man may enjoy company, but a real man makes true friends and

treats them like he would like to be treated. Remember your Oath? It's to remind you and to prepare you for becoming a real man.

See a pattern here? Great! The day you realize that being a man is only a small part genetics and a large part attitude, congratulations! You are well on your way!

JOURNEY AWARD

This is a joining award for the Adventurers program

If you're bridging from the Navigators program, then complete the following:

Traditions:

_____ ✓ Agree to live by the Trailman Oath.

_____ Give your Patrol Leader's name, patrol name, and patrol yell.

Leader Conference:

_____ Discuss Troop safety.

_____ Discuss advancement program.

If you are a new member of the Trail Life USA program, complete the following:

Traditions:

_____ Memorize and agree to live by the Trailman Oath.

_____ Memorize the Trailman Motto.

_____ Demonstrate the Trailman sign and describe when to use it.

_____ Demonstrate the Trailman salute and describe when to use it.

_____ Demonstrate the Trailman handshake.

_____ Give your Patrol Leader's name, patrol name, and patrol yell.

Citizenship:

_____ Memorize the Pledge of Allegiance.

_____ Demonstrate properly folding the American flag.

Leader Conference:

_____ Discuss Troop safety.

_____ Discuss advancement program.

_____   _____

Advisor   Date

HORIZON AWARD

Prerequisite: Earn the Journey Award.

Trail Badge Work:

_____ Earn the following nine badges: Aquatics, Camping, Fire Ranger, First Aid, Our Flag, Outdoor Cooking, Ropework, Trail Skills, and Woods Tools.

_____ Earn the following six Horizon Required Trail Badges as an Adventurer: Citizenship, Emergency Preparedness, Family Man, Outdoor Life, and Personal Resources, and any one Fitness Badge (Cycling, Fitness, Hiking, or Swimming).

_____ Earn a total of ten elective Trail Badges including elective Trail Badges earned as a Navigator.

Servant Service:

_____ Complete 20 hours of service for each year since joining the Adventurers level. Record your hours on the service chart in your handbook and have them verified by an adult.

Troop Involvement:

_____ Maintain a level of Troop meeting attendance acceptable to your Advisor (typically 60% or better).

_____ Participate in at least eight Troop activities since becoming an Adventurer, not including regular meetings. Record each activity on the activity chart in your handbook (trips, camp, community outings, etc.) and have them verified by an adult.

Leadership:

Since earning the Journey Award, complete one of the following leadership options:

_____ Serve as a First Officer, Second Officer, Quartermaster or Patrol Leader for a minimum of six months.

_____ Plan and implement program, food, and wilderness travel plans (biking, hiking, paddle craft, etc.) for a camping or high adventure trip approved by your Advisor.

_____ Plan and implement an Adventurers-only high adventure or extended travel experience including, program, food, and travel plans approved by your Advisor.

_____ Plan and implement a unique Troop or unit service project approved by your Advisor.

_____ At five troop meetings, demonstrate your leadership ability by planning and instructing Navigators in significant Trail Badge skills approved by your Advisor or Trail Guide and the Trailmaster.

_____ At five troop meetings, demonstrate your leadership ability by planning and instructing a Woodlands Trail group in significant skills approved by your Advisor or Trail Guide and the Woodlands Trail Ranger.

Mark Your Progress:

_____ Successfully complete an Advancement Conference with your Advisor.

_____ Successfully complete a Board of Review.

_____   _____

Board of Review Chair   Date

FREEDOM AWARD

Prerequisite: Earn the Horizon Award.

Majors and Minors:

Complete Trail Life USA approved Freedom Experiences
in Major and Minor Fields of your choosing. Each Freedom Experience must be
approved by your Advisor before you start. After completing each Freedom
Experience, have a conference with your Advisor for final approval. Record
your progress in the Freedom Experiences Chart in your handbook along with
your Advisor's approvals.

_____ Complete two Freedom Experiences in your Major Field.

_____ Complete one Freedom Experience in a second Field. (This counts
as a Minor)

_____ Complete one Freedom Experience in a third Field. (This counts as
a Minor)

Troop Involvement:

_____ Maintain a level of Troop meeting attendance acceptable to your
Advisor (typically 60% or better).

_____ Participate in at least 16 Troop activities since becoming an
Adventurer, not including regular meetings. Record each activity
on the activity chart in your handbook (trips, camp, community
outings, etc.) and have them verified by an adult.

Faith:

Complete one of the following Faith Building Activity Options and discuss it
with your Advisor or Trail Guide:

_____ The Adventurers Trail Life USA Spiritual Development Award

_____ An Adventurers level Christian Religious Recognition (according to
your denomination)

_____ An Adventurers Trail Life USA approved youth-mentored Group
Discipleship Program, such as the Band of Brothers Program

_____ The Trail Life USA Vanguard Program

Servant Leadership Project:

_____ Complete a Freedom Servant Leadership Project according to the standards in the Freedom Award Procedure Guide.

Mark Your Progress:

_____ Successfully complete an Advancement Conference with your Advisor and Troopmaster.

_____ Successfully complete a Freedom Award Board of Review.

Note: The Freedom Experiences and Faith Building Activity for the Freedom Award may be completed before earning the Horizon Award while an Adventurer.

_____   _____
Board of Review Chair   Date

HORIZON AWARD SERVICE HOURS

Service Type	Date	Hours	Verified by

HORIZON AWARD ACTIVITIES

Activity Type	Date from	Date to	Nights	Verified by

FREEDOM AWARD SERVICE HOURS

Service Type	Date	Hours	Verified by

FREEDOM AWARD ACTIVITES

Activity Type	Date from	Date to	Nights	Verified by

FREEDOM AWARD EXPERIENCES

Major or Minor	Freedom Experience	Advisor prior approval	Date from	Date to	Advisor final approval

GOALS / NOTES

17

READY TRAILMAN REQUIRED
TRAIL BADGES

Ready Trailman Required Trail Badges help you to become ready.

"Ready for what?" you ask. Anything, of course! You'll learn to become comfortable in the water, useful around camp, and prepared to help out with first aid skills should an emergency arise.

Because these skills build upon each other and form the foundation of your future success, make up your mind to learn the skills through and through rather than merely pass the test.

Remember the Trailman Motto: "Walk Worthy!"

AQUATICS

_____ 1. Participate in a Safe Aquatics Method orientation and fulfill the following requirements pursuant to the Safe Aquatics Method.

_____ 2. Complete the Swimming Competency Test at the Swimmer level.

_____ 3. Demonstrate how to properly put on a personal flotation device (PFD), and while wearing the PFD do the following:

    _____ a. Jump feet first into deep water and swim 25 yards.

    _____ b. Demonstrate the heat escape lessening posture (HELP) cold-water survival technique.

    _____ c. With a group, demonstrate the Huddle cold-water survival technique.

_____ 4. Demonstrate the following reach and throw rescues:

    _____ a. Several reach assists including arm, leg, and towel reaches without entering the water and pole or shepherd's crook

    _____ b. Throwing a rescue tube or ring buoy to someone at least 25 feet out in the water

_____ 5. After ensuring the safety of the swimming area, in deep water, do the following:

    _____ a. Tread water for 3 minutes.

    _____ b. Survival float on your stomach for 3 minutes.

    _____ c. Float on your back for 2 minutes.

    _____ d. Demonstrate a feet-first surface dive.

    _____ e. Demonstrate a head-first surface dive, and recover a diving ring or some other object from the pool bottom.

_____ 6. While wearing shoes, long pants, and a long-sleeve shirt over your swimsuit, jump into deep water.

         _____ a. While treading water, remove the shoes and pants.

         _____ b. Inflate your shirt and float long enough to prepare your pants.

         _____ c. Inflate your pants and use them to float for one minute.

_____ 7. Demonstrate that you can continuously swim 200 yards without stopping to rest. While doing so:
- Use at least three of the following five strokes: front crawl, backstroke, sidestroke, breaststroke, and elementary backstroke.
- Swim each of the three selected strokes for at least 50 yards.

_____ 8. Participate in a skill orientation and an open activity for three of the following aquatics activities: Group water game, Swim race, Diving, Snorkeling, Red Cross Jr. Lifeguard, Scuba, Stand-up paddle boarding, Boardsailing, Canoeing, Kayaking, Rowing, Sailing, Peddle boats, Water skiing, Wake boarding, or an alternate water activity approved by your Unit Leader.

_____   _____

Leader's Signature   Date

CAMPING

_____ 1. Explain how to be a good steward and to observe the low impact camping method.

_____ 2. With your troop, unit, patrol or another group of youth, complete the following activities:

    _____ a. At a camping area, explain where the best place to pitch a tent would be and why.

    _____ b. With a buddy or by yourself, correctly pitch a tent.

    _____ c. Take the tent down, correctly fold it, and pack it away.

    _____ d. Explain the proper care for tents.

    _____ e. Correctly pitch a dining fly, tarp, or other type of covering.

_____ 3. Camping equipment

    _____ a. Make a list of personal equipment you should pack on a weekend camping trip for hot, cold, and rainy weather.

    _____ b. Demonstrate on a camping trip that you have packed all your equipment from your list.

_____ 4. Wilderness sanitation

    _____ a. Demonstrate how to dig and cover a proper cat hole for backwoods human excrement disposal using a small or backpacking shovel.

    _____ b. Explain proper disposal methods for toilet paper for your local wilderness area(s).

_____ 5. Spend at least 15 nights camping in a tent or under the stars and participate in assigned cooking, cleanup, and other camping related duties.

_____   _____
Leader's Signature   Date

FIRE RANGER

_____ ____ 1. Explain how being a good steward and observing the low impact camping method applies to fires.

_____ 2. Fire safety

_____ a. Explain the use of buckets, rakes, and shovels in containing a campfire in a certain location.

_____ b. Describe safe places to have a campfire, how to learn local regulations, and how to set up a fire circle.

_____ c. Describe safe vs. unsafe clothing near campfires and open flames.

_____ d. Describe safe vs. unsafe behavior around a campfire.

_____ e. Demonstrate how to put out fire on your clothing, hair, or body.

_____ f. Demonstrate safe striking of stick and book matches and safe use of a lighter.

_____ 3. Fire materials

_____ a. Explain the use and purpose of tinder, kindling, and fuel firewood.

_____ b. Explain why wet, green, and ant/vine-covered wood are unsafe and not good for fires.

_____ c. Describe several types of fire starters that can be made or purchased.

_____ 4. Fire building

_____ a. Demonstrate building at least three different fire-lays and explain when you would use each one.

_____ b. Light one of the fire lays, tend it, and keep it burning until you are done with it.

_____ c. When finished with the fire, demonstrate the proper way to extinguish it to dead-out.

_____   _____

Leader's Signature   Date

FIRST AID

Cardiopulmonary Resuscitation (CPR), Automated External Defibrillator (AED) Use, and Choking First Aid: *Do either requirement 1 or requirement 2*

_____ 1. Certification

    _____ a. Complete a CPR-AED instruction class taught by the American Heart Association, American Red Cross, or Emergency Care and Safety Institute that includes skill practice with CPR dummies and a teaching AED and teaches these three skill sets:

        i. Adult CPR, AED, and choking

        ii. Child CPR, AED, and choking

        iii. Infant CPR and choking

    _____ b. Find out if your meeting location has an AED and where it is located.

_____ 2. Self-study

    _____ a. Explain Hands-only CPR.

    _____ b. Stopped breathing.

    _____ c. Explain the use of an AED.

    _____ d. Find out if your meeting location has an AED and where it is located.

    _____ e. Describe and show how to tell if someone is choking and when intervention is required.

    _____ f. Describe and show the positions for treating choking in an adult, pregnant woman, child, and infant.

Basic First Aid: *Do either requirement 3 or requirements 4 through 10*

_____ 3. Complete a basic First Aid class taught by the American Heart Association, American Red Cross, or Emergency Care and Safety Institute that includes a hands-on skills session.

_____ 4. Demonstrate the following first aid emergency action plan basics.

    _____ a. Checking the scene

    _____ b. Calling for Help (911 or Poison Control)

_____ c. Approaching safely

_____ d. Providing urgent treatment

_____ e. Triage

_____ f. Treating for shock

_____ g. Deciding the next steps

_____ 5. Demonstrate the following rescuer safety precautions:

_____ a. Wearing of eye protection, breathing mask, and vinyl gloves

_____ b. Proper glove removal

_____ c. Proper hand washing

_____ 6. Explain the symptoms and first aid for the following Sudden Illness Emergencies:

_____ a. Heart Attack

_____ b. Fainting

_____ c. Low blood sugar

_____ d. Stroke

_____ e. Seizure

_____ f. Shock

_____ g. Poisoning

_____ 7. Explain and demonstrate the first aid response for the following:

_____ a. Severe bleeding on a leg and arm

_____ b. Nosebleed

_____ c. Head, neck, and spine injuries

_____ d. Broken bones, including splinting

_____ 8. Explain the First Aid response for the following injuries:

_____ a. Severe bleeding you cannot stop with direct pressure

_____ b. Bleeding from mouth

_____ c. Tooth injuries

_____ d. Eye injuries

_____ e. Penetrating and puncturing objects

_____ f. Internal bleeding

_____ g. Burns (first, second, and third degree)

_____ h. Electric shock injuries

_____ 9. Explain the first aid for the following bites and stings:

       _____ a. Animal and human bites

       _____ b. Snakebites

       _____ c. Insect, bee, and spider bites and stings

       _____ d. Poisonous spider and scorpion bites and stings

       _____ e. Ticks

_____ 10. Explain the first aid for the following temperature-related emergencies:

       _____ a. Heat cramps

       _____ b. Heat exhaustion

       _____ c. Heatstroke

       _____ d. Frostbite

       _____ e. Hypothermia

Trail Life USA First Aid Addendum: *Do requirements 11 through 18.*

_____ 11. Explain and demonstrate first aid for the common outdoor injuries listed below:

       _____ a. Cuts and scrapes

       _____ b. Splinters

       _____ c. Blisters

       _____ d. Something in your eye

       _____ e. Sunburn

       _____ f. Poisonous plants

       _____ g. Dehydration

_____ 12. Explain how the following methods help prevent common outdoor injuries and emergencies:

       _____ a. Work gloves, mole skin, adhesive tape (splinters and blisters)

       _____ b. Sunscreen, sunglasses, broad-brimmed hats

       _____ c. Long pants and long-sleeved shirts

       _____ d. Insect repellent

       _____ e. Plenty of water and a water filter

       _____ f. Synthetic insulating layers and nylon/Gore-Tex outer wear

       _____ g. Sturdy well-fitting hiking boots/shoes

_____ 13. Explain why sun protection is especially important while on the water, in the snow, or at high altitude.

_____ 14. Make first aid kits yourself:

    _____ a. Make a personal first aid kit for hiking and other wilderness trips.

    _____ b. Make a home first aid kit for your family.

_____ 15. Explain how to get medical assistance while on a wilderness camping trip, a river trip, and on open water.

_____ 16. Demonstrate splinting, slings, and bandaging for the following injuries to permit transport of victims:

    _____ a. Twisted ankle (sprain or strain)

    _____ b. Broken ankle

    _____ c. Broken lower arm

    _____ d. Broken upper arm

    _____ e. Broken collarbone

    _____ f. Broken lower leg

    _____ g. Broken upper leg

_____ 17. Demonstrate the following methods of transporting victims:

    _____ a. Walking assists: one and two rescuers

    _____ b. Drags: Blanket, shoulder, and ankle (conduct these with great care)

    _____ c. Two Rescuer Carries: Two-hand seat, four-hand seats, and chair carry

    _____ d. Human stretcher carry for 3-6 Trailmen

    _____ e. Improvised Stretchers: Blanket and shirt/coat (2)

_____ 18. Demonstrate the emergency procedures for the following clothing fire emergencies:

    _____ a. Stop, Drop, and Roll response to your clothes catching fire.

    _____ b. Response to another person who panics and runs.

_____   _____

Leader's Signature   Date

OUR FLAG

Do all of requirements I through 6:

_✓_ I. Basic flag ceremonies:

    _✓_ a. Demonstrate proper folding of the American flag.

    _✓_ b. Demonstrate the proper placement of hands (and hats) while reciting the Pledge.

    _✓_ c. Demonstrate displaying the colors for an outdoor flag ceremony.

    _✓_ d. Demonstrate raising and lowering the American flag for an outdoor flag ceremony.

    _✓_ e. Participate in a flag ceremony for your Troop meeting, award ceremony or other indoor ceremony.

_✓_ 2. Know the Flag Code and its history. Diagram the proper way to display the American flag in the following circumstances:

    _✓_ a. When carried in a procession with another flag or flags

    _✓_ b. When displayed with another flag against a wall with crossed staffs

    _✓_ c. When a number of flags on staffs are displayed with the American flag

    _✓_ d. When state flags or other pennants are flown from the same halyard with the American flag

    _✓_ e. When flags of two or more nations are displayed

    _✓_ f. When a flag is displayed on a staff projecting horizontally from a windowsill or building

    _✓_ g. When the flag is not on a staff and is displayed flat against a wall horizontally and vertically

    _✓_ h. When used on a speaker's platform

    _✓_ i. When flown at half-staff

    _✓_ j. When used to cover a casket

_____ 3. Make a diagram of the American flag, labeling all its parts. Include and be able to define the hoist, peak, fly, staff, halyard, and union.

_____ 4. Learn the history of the Pledge of Allegiance.

_____ 5. Learn the date, the conflict, the American flag's design, its physical condition, and the situation that prompted Francis Scott Key to write the Star Spangled Banner.

_____ 6. Read through the words of the National Anthem written by Francis Scott Key. Explain line by line in your own words what was going on and his views on it.

Do three requirements from group 7 through 15: ↑

_____ 7. Participate in the color guard for a flag ceremony for a community event.

_____ 8. Participate in the color guard for an outdoor flag ceremony.

_____ 9. Find a script giving a meaning or symbolism to each of the 13 folds required to properly fold an American flag and use it in a flag ceremony.

_____ 10. Find or write a special flag ceremony and perform it in front of an audience.

_____ 11. Teach a Woodlands Unit a flag ceremony and help them perform it at a Troop function.

_____ 12. Find or write a respectful American flag retirement ceremony and perform it at a campfire program.

_____ 13. Participate in a flag planting service project at a cemetery for their Memorial Day service honoring veterans.

_____ 14. Learn the history and usage of the 21-Gun Salute.

_____ 15. Research the origins of Flag Day and plan a special event celebrating the day for your Troop or community.

_____   _____
Leader's Signature   Date

OUTDOOR COOKING

_____ 1. Explain how being a good steward and observing the low impact camping method applies to outdoor cooking.

_____ 2. Demonstrate the following:

    _____ a. Sanitation practices

    _____ b. Washing dishes

    _____ c. Personal hygiene

    _____ d. Food Storage

    _____ e. Protecting your food from animals

_____ 3. Explain the advantages, disadvantages, and safety for using propane/butane camp stoves, liquid fuel stoves, lightweight stoves, wood fires, and charcoal.

_____ 4. Set-up, light, and use a lightweight camp stove.

_____ 5. Cook a one-pot meal over the fire or camp stove.

_____ 6. Cook a foil meal on charcoal.

_____ 7. Plan or help plan a balanced nutritious menu for a weekend camping trip.

_____ 8. Purchase the food items needed for a weekend camping trip within the budget set by your leader.

_____ 9. With a buddy or by yourself, prepare, cook, and clean up the planned meals using any of the following means: Campfire, propane stove, liquid fuel stove, charcoal, Dutch oven, sandwich irons, box oven, or solar cooker/oven.

_____   _____

Leader's Signature   Date

ROPEWORK

_____ 1. Explain how being a good steward and observing the low impact camping method applies to Ropework.

_____ 2. Whipping and fusing:

    _____ a. Demonstrate whipping the ends of a natural fiber rope.

    _____ b. Demonstrate fusing the ends of a synthetic rope.

_____ 3. Tie the following knots and describe their usefulness:

    _____ a. square knot

    _____ b. bowline

    _____ c. two half-hitches

    _____ d. taut line hitch

    _____ e. clove hitch

    _____ f. timber hitch

_____ 4. Lashing

    _____ a. Tie square, diagonal, shear, tripod, round, and floor lashings and describe their function.

    _____ b. Lash the following trestles: X-Trestle, A-Trestle, and H-Trestle.

    _____ c. Make a useful structure for camp using at least three different types of lashings.

_____   _____

Leader's Signature   Date

TRAIL SKILLS

_____ I.   Trail ethics:

    _____ a. Explain how being a good steward and observing the low impact camping method applies to Trail Skills.

    _____ b. Explain the Hiker's Code and how a hiker should be responsible and learn the buddy system.

_____ 2.   Trail safety:

    _____ a. Describe how to identify poisonous plants in your area such as poison ivy, poison oak, poison sumac, stinging nettle, and Flowering Poodle Dog Brush (Sticky Nama).

    _____ b. Describe how to identify venomous snakes in your area such as rattlesnakes, coral snakes, or water moccasins.

    _____ c. Describe natural hazards you might encounter on a hike including river crossings and what to do if faced with them.

_____ 3.   Equipment:

    _____ a. Describe the clothing necessary for hiking, including proper footwear and socks.

    _____ b. Explain the limits on how much weight you should carry and how much water you should take.

    _____ c. Demonstrate proper packing and necessary items for a day pack for a day hike.

_____ 4.   Navigation:

    _____ a. Explain how an orienteering compass works.

    _____ b. Explain what a topographic map is and what the contour lines and map symbols mean.

    _____ c. Show how to hold an orienteering compass and take a reading.

    _____ d. With an orienteering compass, orient a map to North.

    _____ e. With an orienteering compass and a topographical map, show one method of adjusting for magnetic declination.

    _____ f. With an orienteering compass and a topographical map, demonstrate finding your location using bearings to landmarks.

_____ 5. Measurements:

    _____ a. Measure the average length of your pace.

    _____ b. Using pacing and the felling method, measure the height of a building, tree, flagpole, or other tall feature.

    _____ c. Demonstrate course direction finding in daylight or moonlight without a compass or GPS receiver.

_____ 6. Do one of the following options:

    _____ a. Complete an orienteering course of at least I mile and 5 stations.

    _____ b. Complete a compass course of at least one mile and 8 bearings.

_____ 7. Using a map and compass together, take a five-mile hike with your patrol or troop.

_____   _____

Leader's Signature   Date

WOODS TOOLS

_____ 1. Explain how being a good steward and observing the low impact camping method applies to Woods Tools.

_____ 2. Describe the Woods Tools Safety Rules

_____ 3. Demonstrate how to clean and sharpen a pocketknife.

_____ 4. Demonstrate how to clean, stow/cover, and change a saw blade for either a folding or bow saw.

_____ 5. Demonstrate cleaning and sharpening an ax or hatchet.

_____ 6. Following the Woods Tools Safety Rules, participate in skill instruction as needed and do three of the following requirements using a knife, bow saw, folding saw, hatchet, or ax:

    _____ a. Whittle a cooking stick and cook a food item over a wood or charcoal fire.

    _____ b. Whittle something out of soft wood.

    _____ c. Make a fuzz stick.

    _____ d. Prepare tinder, kindling, and fuel wood for a small fire.

    _____ e. Saw off a piece of a log at least 2-inches in diameter.

    _____ f. Chop through a log at least 2-inches in diameter on a chopping block.

    _____ g. Split a log.

    _____ h. Limb a log (stand on the opposite side of the log from where you are limbing).

    _____ i. Use an ax to cut a V-shaped notch at least 2-inches deep in a large log (bucking).

_____   _____

Leader's Signature   Date

CHAPTER

18

HORIZON REQUIRED
TRAIL BADGES

Horizon Required Trail Badges carry forward the outdoor skills you learned for Ready Trailman, but they also look forward to the man you are becoming. Because they are written as a mature preparation for manhood, these Trail Badges can only be earned while a member of Adventurers. Citizenship and household skills enter the picture, as does emergency preparedness. These badges challenge ninth and tenth graders with adult concerns, topics, and responsibilities to prepare them for adulthood a scant few years away.

Some of these skills are classed as "Fitness Badges." These are designed to increase your fitness over time and are progressive in nature, meaning they get more difficult as you progress. You are only required to do one of the Fitness Badges (Cycling, Fitness, Hiking, or Swimming).

The other required badges were designed to be worked together as a group so you could conceivably set up a 2-year rotation of 3 badges each year to work on the group requirements together at meetings. A significant chunk of the time on these badges can be done in the regular Adventurer Unit or Patrol meetings.

Citizenship, Family Man, Outdoor Life, and Personal Resources were designed with many options in the learn-by-doing activities and are not as lengthy as they might appear at first glance. Additional options may be published on the Trail Life USA web site as they are approved for the next edition of the Handbook.

CITIZENSHIP

_____ 1. Political and economic systems:

    _____ a. Define the following political systems: democracy, republic, autocracy, and oligarchy.

    _____ b. Define the following economic systems: capitalism, socialism, and communism.

    _____ c. Name a country that practices each type of political system and a country that practices each type of economic system.

    _____ d. Select one of the above countries with a non-constitutional form of government and contrast the treatment of its citizens and noncitizens with the treatment of citizens and noncitizens in the United States (US).

_____ 2. Read the US Constitution and all its amendments and then do the following:

    _____ a. Describe the three different branches of our federal government and explain their respective functions.

    _____ b. Find one federal program or service that is a constitutional function of the federal government and explain why it should be provided at the federal level.

    _____ c. Find one federal program or service that is not a constitutional function of the federal government and explain why it should be provided at the state or local level.

    _____ d. Explain how the Electoral College is used to elect the president and how that differs from the popular vote.

    _____ e. Explain the following constitutional principles: popular sovereignty, limited government, separation of powers, checks and balances, judicial review, and federalism.

    _____ f. Discuss the Bill of Rights, the rights we are guaranteed as citizens of the United States, and the circumstances under which a citizen can lose some of those rights.

_____ 3. Explain the responsibilities of US citizenship.

4. Investigate US citizenship and naturalization requirements using US Citizenship and Immigration Service publications or their web site and do the following:

    a. List the criteria for automatic US citizenship.

    b. List the qualifications to become a naturalized US citizen.

5. Do the following requirements on international treaties:

    a. Explain how international treaties are negotiated, signed, and ratified.

    b. Describe the authority of ratified treaties in US law (US Constitution, Article VI).

    c. Investigate the issues involved in one controversial treaty that the US has signed, but has not ratified.[1]

    d. Present an argument either in favor or against ratification of your selected treaty.

6. Do the following requirements on local, county, and state governments:

    a. Determine the types of local and county government used where you live.

    b. List any major differences of your state government structure relative to the federal government structure.[2]

    c. List at least five services or programs provided for citizens by each of your local, county, and state governments (at least five for each level of government).[3]

    d. List the major taxes and fees collected by your local, county, and state governments to pay for the services they provide.

---

[1] Examples of such treaties include the United Nations (UN) Convention on the Rights of the Child, the UN Convention on the Rights of Persons with Disabilities, the UN Convention on the Elimination of All Forms of Discrimination against Women, and the UN Framework Convention on Climate Change.

[2] Examples include single-house legislature, direct election of judges, periodic confirmation of judges by direct election, etc.

[3] Possible services include street repair, snow removal, trash collection and recycling, police and fire protection, parks and related facilities, educational programs, community swimming pools, tennis courts, skating rinks, stop signs and traffic lights, libraries and medical centers.

_____ e. Explain jury duty, the county juror selection process, and the citizen's duty to serve.

_____ f. List the residency, age, and registration requirements to vote where you live.

_____ 7. Do three of the following citizenship activities:

_____ a. Examine the list of 100 Civics Questions from the US Citizenship and Immigration Services. Prepare for and pass the exam as given by USCIS (Answer 6 out of 10 questions picked at random from the 100 questions).

_____ b. List the federal taxes that citizens may be required to pay and explain how each is assessed and collected. Compare federal government income with expenses for the last year reported.

_____ c. Describe how a bill is written, passed in Congress or your state legislature, and signed into law.

_____ d. List your elected representatives in local, county, state and Federal governments. Select one representative and one issue you care about. Examine his voting record on that issue. Communicate with your representative by email, letter, fax, phone, or in person to express your support or disagreement with his position.

_____ e. List three important local, state, or national political issues for which Biblical moral principles directly apply. Name a bill currently in the local government, state legislature, or US Congress that addresses at least one of these issues. List at least three arguments supporting the bill and at least three arguments opposing the bill.

_____ f. Explain the differences between and the relationship of government debt and budget deficit. For your local, county, state, and federal governments, determine the amount of debt and budget deficit at the end of their last reported fiscal year.

_____ g. Attend a meeting of your local government, county government, school board, or park board. Discuss some of the agenda items that are discussed, voted on, or opened to the public for community comments

_____ h. Participate in a debate of an issue of importance on a local, state, or national level.

_____ i. Visit your state capital and sit in on a legislative session.

_____ j. Visit Washington D.C. and sit in on a legislative session.

_____ k. Visit national landmarks in Washington D.C. such as the Capitol, Library of Congress, National Archives, Washington Monument, or Jefferson Memorial, Lincoln Memorial, World War II Memorial, Korean War Memorial, or Vietnam War Memorial.

_____   _____
Leader's Signature   Date

CYCLING (FITNESS BADGE)

A certified bicycle helmet is required and must be worn for each ride completed for this badge.

_____ I. Do the following:

_____ a. Demonstrate how to determine the proper seat height and bike height.

_____ b. Explain the different sizes and types of tires and when they might be used.

_____ c. Discuss the different types of bicycles.

_____ d. Compare the cost between different types of bikes.

_____ e. Discuss what type of clothing, shoes or equipment should be worn while cycling.

_____ f. Discuss where it is proper and improper to go cycling.

_____ g. Explain the traffic laws for bicycles in your state. Compare them with motor vehicle laws.

_____ 2. Discuss what types of foods and beverages should be consumed before, during, and after a long bike ride.

_____ 3. Go on a ride with others including your leader and demonstrate the following:

_____ a. Mounting, dismounting, steering, pedaling, stopping, and hand signals

_____ b. Proper riding location on the side of the road and along parked cars

_____ c. Gearing, pedaling on ascents and descents, and emergency stops

_____ d. Turns, turn signals, left turn from the center of the street and the alternate left turn technique

_____ e. Crossing of streets and railroad tracks and avoiding obstacles

_____ 4. Demonstrate how to perform basic bicycle repairs:

_____ a. Inflating tires

_____ b. Repairing and/or replacing a tire

          _____ c. Replacing a chain on the sprocket

          _____ d. Adjusting brakes

          _____ e. Raising and lowering the seat

_____ 5. Make a bicycle repair kit for your rides that includes those items necessary to make the repairs listed in the previous requirement.

_____ 6. Outline a training plan of at least three months for improving your fitness using one of the options below to be accomplished within one year. It should include progressive improvement goals and frequency schedule for practice. It must be based on your ability and take into account your current cycling fitness. It must be approved by your leader.

_____ **Option 1: Road Biking:** Using a map of your area, plan and take 10 rides with your leader's approval. Map out your course and plan for rest stops. Identify possible problem areas before riding and determine how you will minimize them. The first ride must be at least 5 miles and you must work up to a final ride of at least 50 miles. Each ride must take place on a separate day and must be completed in one day.

_____ **Option 2: Off-road Biking:** Using trail maps, map your course and execute 10 off-road rides with your leader's approval. Identify possible problem areas before riding and determine how to minimize them. The first ride must be at least 2 miles and you must work up to a final ride of at least 20 miles. Each ride must take place on a separate day and must be completed in one day.

_____ **Option 3: Track Cycling, Cyclo-cross or Para-Cycling:** Develop a goal for a cycling event or events based on your current average time and desired improvement, and then complete the event. It must be approved by your leader.

_____   _____

Leader's Signature   Date

EMERGENCY PREPAREDNESS

_____ I. Make a chart assessing your risk for the following emergencies and understand each one and the unique challenges each presents:

Natural:

Flood	Tornado	Hurricane
Winter Storm	Extreme Heat	Earthquake
Volcano	Landslide	Tsunami
Wildfire	Pandemic	

Technological:

Blackout	Hazardous Materials
Nuclear Power Incidents	Household Chemical

Terrorist:

Explosions	Biological Attack
Chemical Attack	Cyber Attack
Nuclear Device	EMP

Person/Property:

Home Fire	Vehicle Accident
Boating Accident	Gas Leak
Burglary	Carbon Monoxide Poisoning
Drowning	Wilderness / Backcountry Accident

_____ 2. Create an emegency plan for your family for the 10 highest risks that you discovered in your research for number I above. Include the following information:

_____ a. Prevention and preparation necessary

_____ b. Reaction during an emergency including alternate communication plans, meeting locations, and alternate methods for daily tasks of the home

_____ c. Special needs to be considered for the elderly, infirm, infants and small children and animals

_____ d. What to do when the immediate danger is passed or in a prolonged evacuation

_____ 3. Create a list of necessary items and quantities for a Basic Disaster Supply Kit for three days and for two weeks for your family. List some additional items you may also want for some of the more serious long term disasters above. Check off the things you currently have on hand and circle those you don't or need more of.

_____ 4. Create lists of emergency items to keep in your car and at work.

_____ 5. List the local warning systems are available in your area.

_____ 6. Describe the emergency plans are in place at your school, your church, your meeting location, and your workplace (if applicable).

_____ 7. Explain the following emergency water treatment methods: chlorination, distillation, boiling, and filtering.

_____ 8. Present the information you learned in this badge to your family.

_____   _____
Leader's Signature   Date

FAMILY MAN

Family Man Forums:

The Family Man Forums requirements can be completed in part or in full by independent study, with your family or parents, with your Mentor and others, with your Unit, or in a group communicating via the Internet (e.g. video-conferencing).

One option to complete the requirements is to participate in forums with members of your Unit and their fathers on each of the topics below. In a forum, every one studies up beforehand and then they discuss the issues. Rotate the forum facilitator for each topic.

_____ 1. **Family Foundation** *(Reference Gen. 1:28, 2:24; Exo. 20:12-17; Prov. 5:18-19; 1 Cor. 7:2-4, 10-11; Eph. 5:25-31, 6:1-4)*

      _____ a. What is a family?

      _____ b. Why is a man an important part of his family?

      _____ c. How does popular culture undermine the male role in families?

      _____ d. What moral precepts are prescribed for healthy families?

      _____ e. How does popular culture undermine these moral precepts?

      _____ f. How do families benefit men, women, and children?

      _____ g. How do families benefit society?

_____ 2. **Servant Leadership** *(Reference John 13:1-5, 12-17; Tit. 1:6-9; Ch. 1 of this handbook)*

      _____ a. Explain the concept of servant leadership.

      _____ b. Discuss several examples of servant leadership in the Troop(s) or Unit(s).

      _____ c. Discuss several examples of servant leadership in your families.

      _____ d. Brainstorm implementations of servant leadership as future fathers.

_____ 3. **Family Fitness** *(Reference Ch. 5 of this handbook; Exo. 20:2-17; Matt. 7:12, 22:36-40; Rom. 12:2, 13:9-10; 1 Cor. 6:12-20; Gal. 5:16-26; Eph. 6:10-18)*

      _____ a. Discuss the meaning and importance of the four types of fitness: Emotional, Mental, Moral, Physical.

      _____ b. Develop a list of activities to aid the fitness of family members in each of the four types.

Family Activities

Do one activity from each of the following four categories:

_____ **Category I: Nutrition Using the Federal Food Guidelines** *(Reference "My Plate," "Food Pyramid," or another equivalent balanced nutrition plan)* – Do one of a, b, or c

      _____ a. Learn about the food guidelines.

          i. Determine the daily caloric needs are for someone of your age and weight.

          ii. Determine how much water should you be drinking each day and why.

          iii. Write down everything you eat and drink for one week.

          iv. Plan a menu of healthy meals for three days.

      _____ b. Learn the relationship between your diet and good health.

          i. Explain the food guidelines and causes of obesity in childhood and among teenagers.

          ii. List ways to avoid obesity, including diet and exercise.

          iii. Plan one week of healthy menus for your family.

          iv. Select one of your nutritious meals and prepare it for your family and clean up afterwards.

      _____ c. Learn about the food guidelines and plan balanced meals for your family for one day including breakfast, lunch and dinner.

          i. Prepare a list of needed ingredients.

      ii. Show your menus and ingredients list to your Leader.

      iii. Prepare the planned breakfast, lunch, dinner on one day.

      iv. Clean up after each meal.

_____ **Category 2: Household Tasks** – Do either a or b

_____ a. Perform all of the following:

      i. Learn the proper way to do at least five household tasks and perform them for at least one month. These are in addition to grocery shopping, laundry, and ironing task required for ii-iv below. See Sample Household Tasks below for ideas.

      ii. Help your family with the grocery shopping for one week including bagging the groceries, carrying them in, and putting them away properly.

      iii. Learn how to do laundry and do the laundry for yourself or your family for a week.

      iv. Learn how to use an iron and the appropriate temperatures for different fabrics. Press at least three items including something with sleeves.

_____ b. With your parents, agree on at least five recurring household tasks. Track your household tasks for three months on a tracking log. See Sample Household Tasks below for ideas.

Sample Household Tasks

Make the bed	Change bed sheets
Dust furniture	Polish furniture
Clean light fixtures	Clean blinds
Vacuum upholstery	Vacuum floor
Sweep floor	Mop a floor
Clean the bathroom	Set the table
Pack lunches	Wash the dishes
Dry, put away dishes	Load, unload dishwasher
Clean out refrigerator	Defrost freezer

Carry in and put away groceries	Clean an oven
Launder curtains if washable	Sort or fold laundry
Wash the car	Wax the car
Clean inside your car	Cut the grass
Water the grass or garden	Weed a garden
Take out trash	Do the family recycling
Wash windows	Shampoo a carpet
Water house plants	

_____ **Category 3: Family Projects** – Do one of a, b, or c

_____ a. Help your family with a family project. This could be a maintenance activity such as spring landscaping or spring-cleaning. Or it might be a new project such as painting a room or redecorating. List the role of each family member in the project completion.

_____ b. Work with your family to clean out the basement or garage. Sort items into three categories: Things to Keep, Things to Donate, and Things for the Trash. Reorganize as needed as you return items to the space. Take your donated items to a charity and the rest to the trashcan.

_____ c. Perform a community service project with your family. Some examples are to: Participate in a church service day project, help clean up your church or school, plant trees or flowers in a public area and care for them, plan, cook, and deliver a meal to someone in need, do yard work for someone in need, visit the elderly or disabled, or set-up a recycling drive and donate the proceeds to charity.

_____ **Category 4: Family Communication** – Do one of a, b, c, or d

_____ a. Plan a celebration, holiday party or special outing for your family and help to implement it. Include in the plan any costs involved for supplies, invitations, food, preparations, cleaning, transportation, lodging, or needed equipment. Discuss with your family any changes you would make if you were to do it again.

_____ b. Plan and participate in a family meeting. Set ground rules, such as to respect all opinions and to have everyone attend and be allowed to share input. Discuss issues important to your family. For example, decide how chores will be completed, discuss vacation ideas and options, plan a family night or find solutions to a problem.

_____ c. Help a sibling or (under an adult's guidance) a younger child with homework for a week.

_____ d. Under an adult's guidance, read to a younger child each day for a week.

_____   _____
Leader's Signature   Date

FITNESS (FITNESS BADGE)

_____ 1. Research exercises to improve your physical fitness including stretches, strength training and cardiovascular activities. Know the safety guidelines for each activity and at what age it is safe to start them. Make note of each of the exercises, and what muscle or muscle group is being targeted.

_____ 2. Discuss what types of foods and beverages should be consumed before and after a hard workout.

_____ 3. Know how to check and figure your heart rate and know why it is important.

_____ 4. Outline a training plan for improving your fitness based on your research to be accomplished within one year and lasting at least 3 months. It should include progressive improvement goals and frequency schedule for exercise. It must be based on your ability and take into account your current fitness level. It must include strength training goals, cardiovascular training goals, and warm-up and cool-down activities and cover all major muscle groups. It must be approved by your leader and your parents before beginning.

_____   _____

Leader's Signature   Date

HIKING (FITNESS BADGE)

_____ 1. Review the Hikers Code.

_____ 2. Research the proper food for extended hiking outings. Research the amount of food and water necessary for extended hiking outings.

_____ 3. Review other items needed in your pack for an all day hike.

_____ 4. Research exercises, stretches and aerobic activities designed specifically for hiking conditioning.

_____ 5. Prepare a hiking fitness and training plan of at least three months to prepare you for increasing hike lengths based on your research and review it with your leader. Include a training schedule and plans for warm-up, stretching, hiking or other conditioning and a cool down.

_____ 6. Complete a progressive hiking program consisting of at least 10 hikes beginning at 5 miles for the first hike and increasing to at least a 20 mile hike. Prepare a hiking plan for each hike using the Hikers Code including a trail map or route. Provide it to your leader before each trip. Hikes must be completed in one day and all 10 hikes must be completed in one year. Make sure you take into account temperatures, humidity, and other factors that could prove dangerous for hiking.

Elevation Adjustment: 1,000 foot elevation gain = add 1.5 miles
Example: 7 miles with a 2,000 foot gain (1.5*2=3) = 10 miles adjusted total.

_____   _____
Leader's Signature   Date

OUTDOOR LIFE

_____ 1. Explain why weather, water, and lay of the land are important when choosing and setting up camp.

_____ 2. Describe and demonstrate methods to secure food from wild animals, bad weather, and spoilage.

_____ 3. Discuss the importance of safe, clean water and learn how to identify safe or unsafe water. Learn and demonstrate at least two methods of water purification.

_____ 4. Design and pitch a shelter or lean-to using only a tarp and rope. You may fashion your own stakes from wood found at the site. Design your own bedding using natural items and a ground cloth.

_____ 5. Plan a campout for your Unit with an individual equipment list, a group equipment list, duty roster, and activity/program plan.

_____ 6. While a Navigator or Adventurer, spend at least 40 nights camping in a tent or under the stars. Participate in assigned cooking, clean-up and other camping duties. This includes the 15 nights for Camping Trail badge.

Outdoor Life Activity Options

While an Adventurer, do any five of the following 30 activities below. They can be from any of the following topics (duplicate credit for work on other Trail Badges is not permitted):

Adventure Activities

_____ 1. Ascend a mountain to reach the summit requiring at least 10 equivalent miles and gaining at least 1,000 feet in elevation. (for day hiking each 1,000 feet of elevation gain is equivalent to 1.5 additional miles)

_____ 2. Day hike at least 10 equivalent miles. (for day hiking each 1,000 feet of elevation gain is equivalent to 1.5 additional miles)

_____ 3. Backpack (camping at least one night) covering a total of 10 equivalent miles (for backpacking, each 1,000 feet of elevation gain is equivalent to 2 additional miles).

_____ 4. Snow shoe at least 5 miles

_____ 5. Cross country ski at least 5 miles

_____ 6. Camp overnight in the snow (winter camping)

_____ 7. Take a paddle craft day trip of at least 5 hours paddling and requiring the packing of one meal to eat en route.

_____ 8. Go on a paddle craft overnighter such as a canoe trip for a total of at least 10 miles.

_____ 9. Go on a road bike ride of at least 35 miles.

_____ 10. Go on a mountain bike trail ride of at least 15 miles.

_____ 11. Go on a road bike camping trip of at least 20 total miles and 1 night camping

_____ 12. Go on a mountain bike camping trip of at least 5 total miles and 1 night camping

_____ 13. Participate in an approved rock climbing day with at least 4 climbs, one rappel, with one climb being at least a 5.6 on the Yosemite Decimal System (YDS) rating system.

_____ 14. Go camping at least overnight and sleep under the stars (no tent).

_____ 15. Go on a fishing outing where you cook and eat outdoors what you catch.

_____ 16. Go on a half-day fishing outing in a river, lake or ocean where you fish standing in the water, from shore, or from a pier.

_____ 17. Go on a fishing excursion of at least a half day by boat.

_____ 18. Participate in Challenging Outdoor Personal Experience (COPE) course that includes high elements with a duration of at least 4 hours.

_____ 19. Spend at least a half day doing approved trail maintenance with appropriate adult supervision.

Outdoor Cooking Experiences

_____ 20. Demonstrate to a younger boy or Navigators Unit two things you can cook in either a box oven, Dutch oven or can stove.

_____ 21. Create an Outdoor Meal Cookbook for your troop or add to an existing one, include a minimum of two breakfasts, two dinners, and two desserts. Try out each recipe first.

_____ 22. Cook something in two of the following ways: a paper bag, paper cup, orange peel, or cardboard milk carton.

_____ 23. Using a box oven, prepare and bake a meal and a dessert or bread.

_____ 24. Learn how to use a Dutch oven. Use the Dutch oven to cook a dinner and bake either bread or a dessert.

_____ 25. Plan two-days-worth of meals for a backpacking trip. Keep in mind items that are lightweight and do not require refrigeration or a cooler. Go to the grocery and make a price list for the cost of the items you have planned. Discuss how "re-packaging" your ingredients can help use space more efficiently and divide the weight evenly among participants.

Outdoor Gear

_____ 26. Research at least three different materials for sleeping bag filling. Explain the advantages and disadvantages of each, including weight, insulation, and performance when wet. Present your findings to a Unit in your Troop.

_____ 27. Research warm and cool weather clothing for outdoor activities. Include information about layering, insulation, wicking materials, rain gear, head coverings, and footwear. Present your findings to a Unit in your Troop.

_____ 28. Research types and options when buying a tent for camping and for backpacking. Include information about weight, price, space, weather, extras, and other considerations. Present your findings to a Unit in your Troop.

_____ 29. Make an item of gear from scratch (e.g. drawstring bag)

_____ 30. Make an item of gear from a kit (e.g. gaiters)

_____   _____

Leader's Signature   Date

PERSONAL RESOURCES

Time Management:

Do all Time Management requirements (1-6) below:

_____ 1. Make a prioritized list of activities and tasks for a week.

_____ 2. Make a schedule for that same week showing at least school, church, meal times, exercise, activities, and tasks.

_____ 3. Follow your schedule and check of items on your list.

_____ 4. Write on your schedule notes about which scheduled items went OK and which were delayed or took longer.

_____ 5. Check off items on your list as they are completed and note if they were late or took longer than expected.

_____ 6. Tell your mentor what you learned from this exercise and discuss whether you are more schedule or task-oriented.

Money Management Forums:

The Money Management Forums requirements can be completed in part or in full by independent study, school coursework, with your Mentor and others, with your Unit, or in a group communicating via the Internet (e.g. video-conferencing).

One option to complete the requirements is to complete a biblically-based money-management course for teens, such as Dave Ramsey's Generation Change.

Another option is to participate in forums with members of your Unit on each of the topics below. In a forum, every one studies up beforehand and then they discuss the issues. Rotate the forum facilitator for each topic.

Discuss all topics for each of the four Money Management Forums (1-4) below:

_____ 1. Economic Stewardship Forum Topics:

    _____ a. Concept of stewardship.

    _____ b. Difference between the things you want, the things you need and things you should share.

    _____ c. Danger in finding your value or identity in material things instead of Christ. *(Reference Identity in Christ -*

Gen. 1:26-27; Ps. 139:13-16; Mt. 10:29-31, Materialism and contentment - Mt. 6:19-34 and Phil. 4:11-13)

_____ d. Explain the importance of charitable giving. *(Reference Lev. 27:30 33; Ps. 24:1-6; Mt. 6:1-4; Mk 10:17-25; 2 Cor. 9:6-8)*

_____ 2. Insurance Forum Topics:

       _____ a. What is insurance meant to protect against?

       _____ b. Discuss which of the following types of insurance you need and under what circumstances.

           i. Life and Health Insurance: life, health, disability, accidental death and dismemberment, and long term care.

           ii. Personal Property and Casualty Insurance: home-owners, renters, auto, personal umbrella, recreational vehicle, boat owners, jewelry or other fine arts.

           iii. Business Property and Casualty Insurance: general liability, professional liability, umbrella liability, workers compensation, property, and industry specific policies.

_____ 3. Debt Forum Topics:

       _____ a. Consequences when expenses exceed income and the possible causes being in debt.

       _____ b. Explain these types of debt, their advantages and disadvantages: Mortgage, Auto loan, Home equity loan, Credit card

       _____ c. Why credit card debt is especially dangerous.

       _____ d. Difference between a debit card and a credit card.

       _____ e. Alternatives to going into debt for a purchase.

       _____ f. What steps can be taken to get out of debt.

       _____ g. How a budget helps you to avoid debt.

_____ 4. Investment Forum Topics:

　　　_____ a. Discuss the advantages, disadvantages, and expected
　　　　rates of return for:
　　　　i.　Stocks
　　　　ii.　Bonds
　　　　iii.　Mutual funds
　　　　iv.　Certificates of deposit
　　　　v.　Money market accounts
　　　　vi.　Bank savings accounts
　　　　vii.　Annuities.

Money Management Activities:

Do one activity from each of the three Money Management categories below:

_____ I.　Budgeting – Do one of a, b, or c

　　　_____ a. Pick two jobs or businesses
　　　　i.　Compute the cost to get into that job (school, training,
　　　　　tools, equipment, business start-up costs, etc.)
　　　　ii.　Determine pay or typical net income
　　　　iii.　Ignoring interest, determine how long it takes to
　　　　　earn back your start-up costs using 25% of income
　　　　iv.　Compare start-up costs and time to pay them back
　　　_____ b. Develop a budget for you as a single 25 year old not
　　　　living at home.
　　　　i.　Pick a job
　　　　ii.　Research average pay
　　　　iii.　Make complete budget including: Housing – rent or
　　　　　mortgage (no more than 25% of gross income),
　　　　　Utilities (electric, gas, phone, Internet, cable, etc.),
　　　　　Food, Clothing, and Hygiene Supplies, Auto (loan
　　　　　payment, gasoline, insurance, maintenance,
　　　　　licensing), Other Transportation (Bus, train, etc.),
　　　　　Health (insurance, doctor/dentist visits, drugs, etc.),
　　　　　Fun (travel, movies, eating out, and other entertain-
　　　　　ment), Education and Training Charitable Giving
　　　　　(church, missions, and other charities), Taxes

(income, FICA, self-employment, property, miscellaneous state taxes)

    iv. Compute the percentage of your gross income budgeted for each category and present in tabular or graphical form (e.g. a pie chart).

_____ c. Develop a three-month budget and track your income and expense.

    i. Create a three-month budget for all of your income and expenses, including spending, saving and giving.

    ii. If you do not have one, and with your parents' permission, set up a checking and a linked savings account to use for this activity.

    iii. Track your actual income and expenses for three months.

    iv. Deposit your saving amount in your savings account and some of your giving or spending amount in your checking account.

    v. During the three months, write several checks, make several deposits, keep a checkbook, and balance your checkbook with the monthly bank statement.

    vi. After one month, explain to your mentor or Troop Leader any deviations from your original plan including unexpected expenses.

    vii. Adjust your budget based on what you learned from the first month.

    viii. At the end of three months, explain any deviations from your adjusted plan including unexpected expenses.

_____ 2. Investments – Do either a or b

_____ a. Play the Virtual Stock Exchange game on marketwatch.com.

    i. Play for about 6-9 months to see some of the long-term effect of the market.

ii. Have your Mentor set up a game for all in your Unit working on this badge or include multiple units to have enough players.

iii. Check at least weekly on your investments and make any adjustments you think will help your portfolio grow.

iv. Discuss the results at the end, comparing how each person did with his strategy.

_____ b. Play the Portfolio on Paper investment game for about 6-9 months.

i. You have $5,000 in pretend money to invest in the stock market.

ii. Investigate companies you would like to invest in.

iii. Create a portfolio on paper or on the computer and track your virtual investment.

iv. You may sell and purchase new stocks as often as you wish but you must deduct $10 each time you do so.

v. At the end of the game, evaluate the income and change in your investment value.

vi. Compare your results with others in your Unit who also complete this exercise.

_____ 3. Debt – Do either a or b

_____ a. Student loan payback analysis

i. Choose a field of study and associated business or career. Determine the current average annual pay for that career or business.

ii. Pick two schools with significantly different annual costs.

iii. Total up those costs and determine a reasonable amount per year you can pay for school.

iv. Assume the remainder is funded with student loans and total the loan amount for each school.

v. Look up the current student loan rate and compute how long it will take to pay each loan back at ten percent of your income.

_____ b. Compute the monthly payment and total interest paid for the following loans and explain what you learned from this exercise.

    i. 15-year mortgage of $100,000 at 5% annual interest (180 monthly payments)

    ii. 30-year mortgage of $100,000 at 5% annual interest (360 monthly payments)

    iii. 15-year payoff of $20,000 credit card debt at 20% annual interest (180 monthly payments)

    iv. 30-year payoff of $20,000 credit card debt at 20% annual interest (360 monthly payments)

Communication:

Do the following Communication requirements (1 and 2) below:

_____ 1. Document one money management activity in a short written report including graphics to communicate the results.

_____ 2. Present the findings of either the same or a different money management activity in a short presentation to your Mentor and Unit.

Leader's Signature	Date

SWIMMING (FITNESS BADGE)

_____ 1. Research exercises to improve your swimming fitness including stretches, strength training and conditioning drills.

_____ 2. Discuss what types of foods and beverages should be consumed before and after a swimming workout. How much should you eat and drink, and why?

_____ 3. Learn and explain the different strokes used in competitive swimming. Learn how improvements to your stroke, kick, and turns can improve your fitness and speed.

_____ 4. Outline a training plan of at least three months for improving your fitness using one of the options below to be accomplished within one year. It should include progressive improvement goals and frequency schedule for practice. It must be based on your ability and take into account your current swimming fitness. It must be approved by your leader.

_____ **Option 1:** Improve your USA Swimming Motivational Time Standard for your age for a specific stroke or strokes (e.g. BB to A).

_____ **Option 2:** Develop a goal for a swim event(s) based on your current average time and desired improvement (e.g. Go from 1:05 in the 100M Free to less than 1 minute).

_____ **Option 3:** Build up endurance to be able to swim a specific distance in a time agreed upon by your leader (e.g. Swim a mile in less than 30 minutes).

_____   _____
Leader's Signature   Date

19

ELECTIVE
TRAIL BADGES

Elective Trail Badges help round out your experience with topics that have personal appeal. Developed Elective Trail Badges are available for downloading for personal use by the owner of this Handbook who is a registered member of Trail Life USA at www.TrailLifeUSATrailBadges.com, but are copyrighted and may not be reproduced or shared.

In addition to these developed Elective Trail Badges, Trailmen can further improve their research and communication skills when they tackle creating a new badge of their own!

DESIGN YOUR OWN BADGE OPTIONS

Trailman (non-adult), you can choose an area of study and design your own Elective Trail Badge! There are three ways to do this (described below). In addition to getting your badge approved by your Troop Advancement Coordinator, you'll need to work with a Trail Badge Mentor and submit your individual Elective Trail Badge design to the home office for final review. Part of earning the badge is designing the steps to complete it, so this method is not intended as a way for Adult Leaders to introduce group badges of their own design, but rather as an educational option in self-directed investigation in an area of individual interest to a non-adult Trailman.

There are a number of ways to design your own badge.

Design Your Own Badge: Analogy

This is one of the easiest ways to draft a "Design Your Own Badge." Simply find an analogous badge and modify it for the new topic. For example, a Kayaking Trail Badge can be derived from the Canoeing Trail Badge.

Design Your Own Badge: Certification

Find a significant certification

(Scuba, Jr. Lifeguarding, etc.), and after getting approval from your adult leader, earn your certification. The certification should take at least 8 hours in order to qualify as a complete elective Trail Badge.

....

Design Your Own Badge: CLEAR Method

Choose, Learn, Explore, Apply, Report (CLEAR) is a formulaic Trail Badge method that will work well for many topics no matter how general or specific. The non-adult Trailman designs a Trail Badge that takes a minimum of 8 hours to complete, and the CLEAR method requires that the Troop Advancement Coordinator or Trail Badge Mentor approves each phase of your badge design. The method is as follows:

Choose
- A topic of interest for your Elective Trail Badge
- A registered adult leader to serve as your Mentor

Learn
- Basic facts and broad concepts of the topic
- The history or development of the topic

Explore
- Details and gain mastery of key elements of the Topic

- Hands-on or practical experience

Apply
- Complete a personal project of at least 3 hours duration (advanced experience, career, certification, group activity, mentoring, or service type requirement)
- Demonstrate acquired knowledge or skills (advanced experience, exam, paper, presentation, or other method approved by your adult leader)

Report
- Trailman submits his Design Your Own Badge Report on the required form to the Trail Life USA Home Office.
- Troop advancement leader documents completion in the online Advancement Module.

DESIGN YOUR OWN BADGE: EXAMPLES

On the following pages are two examples of the CLEAR Method of designing your own Trail Badge. Each of these examples would take at least 8-hours to complete and would result in a Trailman gaining general knowledge and specific mastery of certain components of the chosen topic.

CLEAR Trail Badge Example:

Dutch Oven Cooking

Choose
- Topic: Dutch Oven Cooking
- Mentor: Cowboy Bob (Dr. Robert Owens, Troop Committee member)

Learn
- Learn the basics of Dutch oven cooking and do the following:
  - Estimate cooking temperature from the number of charcoal briquettes on the top and bottom
  - Season a Dutch oven
  - Properly care for and clean a Dutch oven
  - Use Dutch ovens on camp stoves
  - Collect 2 single pot dinner recipes, 2 dessert recipes, and 2 bread recipes
- Learn the early European, Dutch, and American history of Dutch ovens

Explore
- Plan out the needed ingredients, cooking times, and other information for cooking the 6 Dutch oven recipes.
- Cook the 6 Dutch oven recipes

Apply
- Teach Dutch oven cooking basics to the new Navigators.
- Plan and judge a Navigators Dutch oven cooking contest at the church picnic.

Report
- Complete the Design Your Own Badge Report for Dutch Oven Cooking and submit to the Trail Life USA Home Office.
- Troop advancement leader documents completion in the online Advancement Module.

CLEAR Trail Badge Example:

Welding

Choose

- Topic: Welding
- Mentor: Bob Smith (Navigators Trail Guide)

Learn

- Research basic welding information to familiarize yourself with this field
  - List the major types of welding and when they are used.
  - List the safety rules, safety gear and clothing used for welding.
  - List the types of equipment used in welding and their approximate cost to purchase.
  - Explain the proper care and storage of welding equipment, tools, safety gear, and clothing.
- Research the history of welding from antiquity to the present. Identify the major developments on a time line

Explore

- Research stick-welding on-line. List the equipment required and describe the welding process for stick welding. Define welding, electrode, slag, and oxidation. List the steps in the stick-welding process and how the metal is heated. Explain how filler metal welds two pieces of metal, and how molten metal is prevented from oxidizing.
- Arrange a visit and tour of a welding shop. Talk to the owner about the welding business. Have a journeyman welder teach stick-welding techniques and practice those techniques with his assistance.

Apply
- Set up welding equipment with all the safety precautions in place. Have the set-up inspected and approved by your mentor. Weld a sculpture of metal junk art using at least 7 pieces of steel in various shapes such as plate, pipe, I-beam, etc. Decorate the sculpture with weld beads, including forming your initials on a plate in the sculpture.
- Construct a tri-fold display showing the various types of welding processes and their proper applications. Include appropriate pictures, labels and descriptions.

Report
- Complete the Design Your Own Badge Report for Welding and submit to the Trail Life USA Home Office.
- Troop advancement leader documents completion in the online Advancement Module.

Index

PHOTO CREDITS BY PAGE NUMBER